NON-DISCLOSURE

TO HOWARD -

BEST OF HEALTH!

2019

GEORGE DAPRA

outskirts press

This book is dedicated to the loving memory of my late immigrant parents, who sacrificed for their children to have a better life, and to my entire family, including our newest addition, George Eden.

Disclaimer

In 1985, as part of my position as Inspector in the Witness Security Division, United States Marshals Service, I was required to sign a Secrecy Agreement. Years later I also signed a Non-Disclosure Agreement. One of the conditions of the agreements was not to publish information, even after retirement, without the prior approval of the Attorney General of the United States.

After two years I completed my first draft and submitted the manuscript in July of 2015 to the Office of General Counsel for review. I was notified that "Any person who, without the authorization of the Attorney General, knowingly discloses any information received from the Attorney General under paragraph (1) (G) shall be fined $5,000 or imprisoned five years, or both." 18 U.S.C. 3521(b) (3).

No one in my position as an Inspector in New York, in the forty years since the creation of the Program, has ever received permission to publish. It is not my intention to violate any conditions of the agreements I signed. I would never knowingly reveal any sensitive government information that would cause harm to any persons or personnel, relocated witnesses, or the integrity of the Program.

In June of 2016, I received notification that the Department of Justice, Office of Enforcement Operations (OEO) had completed its sensitivity review. Certain items were prohibited from disclosure, and OEO requested sensitive information removed. Therefore, I complied by editing, deleting, and redacting information. My second draft was submitted on June 20th for additional review by the Witness Security Division and the Office of General Counsel.

In December 2016, I received another notification that additional sensitive and operational security information in my second draft needed to be redacted. A scheduled conference call was set up with management personnel in the Witness Security Division. Another review conducted via telephone was completed. In January 2017, I submitted my third and final draft to the Division.

After three draft submissions the following was agreed:

1. My manuscript cannot name current or former DOJ employees associated with the Program.

2. My manuscript cannot name current, former, or deceased Program participants.

As a result, in this book the above-referenced individuals' names are replaced with XXX. In February 2017, I received notification from the Witness Security Division that the final draft was approved.

Table of Contents

Prologue

One early morning in the fall of 1976, I received a call from the front desk manager that Mohammad Ali would be arriving at the Plaza Hotel around 4 AM. I was waiting at the Central Park South entrance. No one was around; it was a quiet morning. Three stretch limousines pulled up to the curb. In the first limo was Ali's business manager, who got out and strolled into the hotel to register. In the second limo was a female with an infant who also went into the hotel. After about ten minutes, Ali, who was sleeping in the third limo, got out and stretched. He was dressed in a gray sweat suit and wearing black combat boots. They had driven down from his training camp upstate in the Catskill Mountains. We exchanged greetings and he said he was going to run in Central Park later. He was quiet and I escorted him into the hotel. The whole party went up to their rooms.

I stayed in the front desk manager's office after talking to him when fifteen minutes later I heard loud screaming in the lobby area. I went out and saw Ali yelling at the white-gloved elevator operator who was sitting in a wingback chair in the lobby. Ali, who was registered up on one of the higher floors, had been ringing for the elevator. The elderly operator was snoozing in the comfortable high-back wing chair and didn't hear the ring. Ali ran down the flights of stairs and was furiously yelling at the operator that his wife and baby were up there in their room and what if there was a fire! They would be in danger! The operator was very apologetic. I went over and said to Ali, "Champ, you want to run in the park?" He started jabbing and we walked out the 59th Street exit. He was mumbling about beating Kenny Norton, whom he was training to fight in an upcoming battle in Yankee Stadium. He was concerned about being mugged in the dark of Central Park. Remember, this was in the 1970s when New York City had a high crime rate and there were highly published reports of muggings and murders in Central Park. I said to him, "No one is going to mug you!"

In the quiet of the early morning, I could hear his boots hitting the pavement as he crossed 59th Street, jogging to the entrance of the park. I stood there at the top of the steps and watched him. I could hear him saying, "Ain't nobody going to mug the Champ!" as he nervously glanced back and forth over his shoulders, throwing jabs into the darkness. I waited a few minutes on the steps as a cool September breeze blew leaves around the street. It was then that I first realized nobody, not even the Heavyweight Champion of the World and one of the greatest of all time, is immune to fear.

There is a small group of men who have embraced a life of fear. They are members of organized crime. Theirs was a more complicated life. They not only had to worry about themselves being killed but also had to deal with the threat of going to jail for their illegal activities. Those who broke with the rules and decided to cooperate with the government and enter the Witness Security Program experienced an additional layer of anxiety. Their testimony in court sealed their death sentences with the mob. Later in this book, you will read about my experiences dealing with these characters in the Program. But first, let's start at the beginning.

1

In The Beginning

Before I came to America, I thought that the streets were paved with gold. When I arrived I learned three things. First, the streets were not paved with gold. Second, the streets were not paved at all. Finally, I was expected to pave them. Only an immigrant can appreciate America.

—Joseph Marchesi, 1919

I am the sixth child, the baby, of Italian immigrants. Before I tell you about me, I want to introduce you to my parents.

On 15 February 1903, my father, Lorenzo (Larry) Dapra, was born in the village of Panchia in the Val di Fiemme, in the Trentino region. Lorenzo was the son of Gilberto Dapra from Panchia and Rose Vanzo Dapra from Cavalese. They immigrated to America from Havre, France, on January 10, 1906, aboard the vessel *La Britannia* and were processed through Ellis Island. They resided at 239 W. 26th St., NY, NY, for a period of time where Gilberto, a stone mason, worked as a "sand hog" digging underground for the construction of NYC subway tunnels. Later they moved up the Hudson River to Highland Falls, New York, where there were other families from the Trentino region. Many of these Italian immigrants were stone masons who were needed for the construction of the stone fortress known as West Point along the cliffs of the majestic Hudson River.

The town is surrounded by the mighty Hudson River to the west; the United States Military Academy at West Point to the north and east, and further to the north the Storm King mountain. The south is bordered by Bear Mountain State Park and Dundenburg Mountain and the Palisades Interstate Park Commission rims southeast. In essence, the town is sandwiched in between mountains and the river. The picturesque Hudson Highlands was a miniature postcard of the Trentino region of Italy where the Dolomite Mountains punctuate the clouds.

On January 20, 1911, my mother, Giacoma (Jenny) Graziano, was born in the small town of Villa Rosa, Sicily. This was the town her father, Salvatore Samual Graziano, was from. He worked in a sulfur mine in the area. Her mother, Marietta Bonsignore Graziano, was from Calascibetta. On March 16, 1921, Jenny emigrated from Naples, Italy, to the United States. She was not alone. Along with her on this unpleasant journey were her mother, sisters Rose and Josephine, and brother Cologero (Lee). Prior to the trip, they stayed on a relative's farm where they drank goat's milk and took in other nourishments in preparation for their long ocean crossing.

Marietta's father passed away just two days prior to the trip. The funeral was the day before their departure. While the family was at the funeral, thieves broke into their house in Sicily and ransacked their belongings, looking for money. It was well-known that the family was going to America. Marietta had hidden the money her husband had been sending her from America for the trip. The thieves left empty-handed.

My grandfather had made the trip a few times before and did not want his family to endure the overcrowding and dreadful experience of going through the Ellis Island Immigration Center. So, with the help of some friends in Boston, he was able to arrange for his family to disembark there and then to continue the journey to New York by car. He made arrangements to meet his family in Boston and to get them off the boat. The family also settled in the small village of Highland Falls, New York, in the Hudson Highlands. Most of these Italian and Sicilian immigrant families all lived in what was known as the Italian section in the middle of the village.

My mother, Jenny, was eleven years old when she started school in America. She was placed in the first grade to learn English. Other kids made fun of her in school because of her poor English. She would go home crying and tell her parents. They removed her from school and kept her at home to help her mother with not only household chores but also the cooking and the care of two additional sisters, Angie and Jo, who were born in America. That was the extent of my mother's formal education. She never returned to school but instead worked her chores and never complained as the years went by and she grew older.

Gilberto, my father's father (1874–1926), died at fifty-two years of age from throat cancer, the result of digging in the construction of the subways and stone dust in the underground of New York City subways. My father's mother, Rosa, raised her son Larry, who became interested in becoming an electrician.

Since my father was born in Northern Italy and my mother was born on the island of Sicily, you may be wondering how they ever got together. Let me tell you their story. A love story for the ages!

My mother's father was a very strict Sicilian. When he would have workers come into his house, he would make sure that his daughters stayed in the back of the house in their rooms so the workers would not see them. One day my father arrived at the house to fix a problem with the electricity. My mother was in her room and the door was ajar. My father was working in the outer room. My mother peeked out the door and their eyes met. My mother was scared and closed the door. After that episode my father would drive by the house and beep his horn to see if my mother would come to the window. However, my grandfather would run to the door and if he saw my father's car, he would run out into the street. My father would take off with my grandfather chasing him down the street cursing at him! My father was still interested in meeting my mother, so he asked his mother, Rosa, to approach my grandfather and request an introduction. Rosa went to my mother's house and asked if she could bring Larry over to meet my mother. My grandfather said "NO!" After a few months another request was made, with the same results. A few months after that, Rosa approached my grandmother to ask her if she could work on my grandfather to allow an introduction. Finally, my grandfather agreed to have my father and his mother over to his house for coffee. Of course, my father had to sit at one end of the table and my mother at the other. There were a few more visits under the same conditions.

My grandfather tried to arrange a marriage for my mother with a wealthy NYC grocery store owner. My mother was not happy and told her mother she did not want to marry this guy but wanted to marry Larry. A few more months passed. My father went to my grandfather and asked to marry my mother. That did not go well. My grandmother had to talk to my grandfather again. Finally, my grandfather gave in and agreed to the marriage. From the time their eyes met for the first time when my father was working in the house till the time they were married, a total of twelve years had passed. The first time they kissed was on the altar of the Sacred Heart Church under the eyes of God during the sacrament of marriage. They were married on June 19, 1938. After their wedding, my grandfather let my father use his Chrysler Imperial to drive Aunt Jemma home. Aunt

Jemma lived in Cleveland, Ohio! That was my parents' honeymoon. My father told me stories that when he was driving in Cleveland, the NY Yankees were playing and kids would throw rocks at the car because of the New York plates. On the way back, they stopped in Niagara Falls. Soon there were six children in eight years. Plus, my mother had had two miscarriages. Larry Jr. was born in 1939, followed by Sal, Lee, Jacque, and Margie, and then I came along, the last to be born. On September 28, 1947, I was christened by Father Hugh Devers in the Church of the Sacred Heart. My godparents were the late Aunt Rose and Uncle Bill.

After I was born my family moved into the house on Mearns Avenue that my father's mother lived in. She occupied the top floor. We referred to her as Nanny Up. Our family now consisted of eight people. I lived with my parents in their room. My two sisters and three brothers all lived in the other room. When Nanny Up passed away in 1955, we all graduated to the roomier upstairs. My parents had their own room, the girls had their own room, and the four boys all lived in one room. It is what it is!

Actually, my parents rarely lived alone. I was the last one in the family to get married and move out of our house. At one point my brother Larry's classmate at West Point, Captain Hank Morris, was assigned to West Point, and he lived with my parents for a while. When my parents became elderly, my sister Jacque and her husband, Lenny, bought the vacant lot next door from my brother Lee and his wife, Carol. Jacque and Lenny expanded the existing house, moved in, and that is where they raised their family of Lenny, Mark, and Krista.

My sisters, brothers, and I all attended the local parochial school, Sacred Heart of Jesus. Every morning before we went to school, we would have to line up on our front porch. Our mother would be standing there with a bottle of cod liver oil. She would give us a spoonful as we ran out the door. If we were good, she would give us a slice of an apple as a treat. My sisters thought it was dreadful, but I didn't mind it. I think back and feel that introduction was my introduction to nutrition. Today, I drink apple cider vinegar just like my father used to.

Our school was run by the Franciscan nuns. We knew all the nuns and they knew all of us personally because my mother's sister, Aunt Jo, was herself a Franciscan, Sister Mary Inez. Right across the street from the school and the church was Ladycliff College, where the nuns lived. Ladycliff has since closed. West Point bought the property and now operates their visitor center, museum, and business offices, etc. on the site. Aunt Jo was stationed in nearby Peekskill at St. Joseph's Orphanage. The main Mother's house and chapel are still there, as are a few nuns. However, they too had to sell off property, and now condos occupy most of that property. My sixth- and seventh-grade teacher, Sister Helen Marie, is still living. She was assigned to a parish in Brooklyn but now is back in Peekskill. Recently, Elaine and I visited her at an open house in Peekskill. My fifth-grade teacher, Sister Francis Anette, is also still living. However, she left the order and now lives in Florida. Aunt Jo also left the order after twenty-eight years because of health reasons. They all keep in touch.

In later life, Aunt Jo would always tell me the story of how when I was very young and our family was visiting her, the nuns would circle around me and pinch my checks and fuss with me. Once I said to them, "Do you know what?" They all stopped to listen to me. I said, "My dad curses!" The nuns were aghast! My mother leaned over to my father and said, "Larry, I told you not to swear in front of the kids."

Aunt Jo also told me that her father used to go to a meat market in Stony Point called Martino's. He would help the Italian immigrants with their paperwork to become citizens. He would also teach them to speak English and how to write. I can still remember his beautiful penmanship.

We lived at the top of a long hill. Along with the other kids in our neighborhood, we were known throughout the town as "The Hilltoppers." It was a lively neighborhood. On the way up the hill, on a side street, sitting on a bluff was a bar called "Hilltop Charlies." My mother's cousin owned the bar. Years later one of my grade school friends, Peter Carroll, operated the bar. He recently told me a story. It was in the winter during a blizzard. The snow was deep and the wind was blowing in all directions. The bar was closed but he was working in there, looking out the window at the falling snow. It was quiet outside and there were no cars on the road. He noticed in the distance a moving object. He was startled at first because he thought it was a ghost! Because of the blizzard he could not make out what it was. Then the object started getting closer and he realized it looked like a person walking, wearing a long coat. Finally, the figure was passing in front of the bar. He recognized the person. It was my mother! He opened the door and yelled out to her and asked her if she wanted a ride. She declined and said she was walking down the hill to church. That describes my mom, a very devoted woman.

There were other families with children in the neighborhood. Everyone hung out in front of our house. We would play a ball game of Up Against the Steps. We would throw a tennis ball against our front steps. If it caught the edge of the step at the right spot and went up over the street, it would fly over Spellman's hedges across the street and that would be a homerun. Later, my brother Sal and his wife, Linda, would buy this house and raise their son, Kenny, a member of the new generation of Hilltoppers, there.

The long, winding street leading up to our area was called Mountain Avenue. When there were heavy rains, snow, or bad stormy weather, our loving mother would arrange for a taxi to pick us up from school since there was no bus transportation. At the end of the school day, over the PA system, an announcement would blare, "The taxi is here for the Dapras." Of course, kids being kids, some of my classmates would ridicule me. And, of course, my siblings and I cringed when the announcement was made, but we were so grateful for the ride!

One of my fondest school memories happened in kindergarten. After the half-day morning session, I would go upstairs to my sister Margie's first-grade class. The first-grade nun would put me in the back of the room, where I would sit and rest my head on the desktop to nap. When I woke up, I would find a Tootsie Roll candy on the desk that the nun had left for me. Some students were afraid of the nuns, but as you can see, I was off to a sweet start!

We grew up in a very Catholic environment. So, having an aunt as a nun, we had to be on our best behavior. In the summer, sometimes after daily Mass we had a ritual: Our mother would walk us up to the Bus Terminal restaurant, where we would sit at the counter and have eggs and toast. That was a real treat.

My brothers and I were all altar boys. When I first started, my oldest brother Larry instructed me in the duties and procedures of serving Mass on the altar. At that time the Mass was in Latin. In the beginning, he would serve with me and show me what to do. We would get up early and walk down the hill to the church for the first Mass of the day. One winter while we were walking to church I asked him a question. I said, "Larry, in the cold mornings when we walk to church and talk, why does smoke come out of our mouth?" He told me, "That's from eating toast." What a funny thing to say! Later in high school I became a Squire in the Knights of Columbus and eventually a Third-Degree Knight.

One of my memories in kindergarten was when a few of us boys were on the floor in the center of the room, building a high sky-scraper with wooden blocks. At our age it seemed taller than any of us. Just then the principal nun arrived at the door, holding the hand of a new student. The nun introduced him and asked us to welcome John Fitzpatrick. Just then John broke free from the nun, ran and knocked down our blocks! That was a start to a long, long friendship with John.

A warm, sunny spring day is the perfect day for young boys to play hooky. In eighth grade I met John, Peter, and some of my other friends in front of the school before class. It was a great morning. We decided to go down to the river by the railroad tracks. We ended up going into a swamp and getting soaked. We took our pants off and let them dry in the sun on a rock ledge, and while we waited, we waved to the trains as they went by. We were lying on the rock, enjoying the sun, when we heard a deep voice out of the blue. "Well, well, well. What do we have here?" It was Monsignor Moody, our parish priest, walking his dog Robespierre. He knew where young boys would be on a warm spring day. We were shocked and jumped up, grabbing our clothes. He told us, "There are a lot of people back at the school who are worried about you boys. I suggest you go back now." We ran.

Once we got back to school, we were sent home. The next day the other boys I was with told me how they had their ears boxed! Another said his behind was so sore, he couldn't sit down. They asked what happened to me. I told them when I got home, my mother gave me a bowl of ice cream and told me, "Don't tell your father!"

That was my mom, sweet, generous, and forgiving. It never occurred to me to be afraid to go home. I knew she would love me anyway. She would always tell us when we were alone with her that we were the best in the family. She would say, "You are the best!" Later on in life when we were all together, we would joke with her and say, "Okay, Mom, now that we are all together, who is the best?" She would respond, "You all are the best!"

My father, not my Sicilian mother, was the fiery one. Man, was he tough. He never wore a coat in the winter until he was in his late seventies. He smoked two packs of Camels a day, drank Rheingold beer, and ate pepperoni regularly. When I was growing up my father did not own a car. I remember he would get a case of beer delivered by the Hub market in town to our back door every week. I would have to stack the empty bottles back into the case for the delivery man. Occasionally, he would chase that beer down with a whiskey if he had company. If he wasn't feeling well, he would make a concoction of apple cider vinegar, lemon, and honey. He was funny and he was fearless and his language was always colorful. He was a volunteer fireman and once in a blizzard without wearing a coat, he hung onto the back of the firetruck responding to a fire. He got frostbite on his hands and chest. Shortly after that he was elected chief of the fire department.

One day the village fire whistle blew. My father ran down the hill to the fire department on Mountain Avenue only to find out that the fire was in his own backyard! My brother Lee was using a magnified glass in the sun to set some leaves on fire. The fire spread to the woods behind our house. I remember Lee running into the house and hiding under his bed. My father was cursing looking for him. My father finally saw Lee's feet sticking out from under the bed. He dragged him out and gave him a good fanning. At that time Lee was the fire department mascot. Naturally, my brothers and I, in turn, were all mascots and led the department in the local holiday parades. I was the mascot in 1954. We were just doing our civic duty and it was a tradition.

In our backyard we had an arbor with rambling grapevines. There was a patio under the grapevines where we would sit in the shade. When the grapes were in season, we would sit and eat them. Across the yard up on a little hill, there was an outhouse. When you went in to use the outhouse, there was a military bomb with numbers on it. It was about two feet long with fins on the tail, just sitting in the corner. I never knew where it came from or what happened to it. I once asked my brothers and they said not to tell anyone about it or show it to anyone. No one ever talked about it. It was just there. Then one day it was gone. My father never said a word about it.

We had some loving, memorable traditions. One began on Saturday. My brothers and I would walk down to my grandfather's house on Center Street in the Italian section to have our hair trimmed. Through their kitchen was a door that led to the basement, where it was always cool and dark. It was an original man cave with my uncle Lee's professional barber's chair down there positioned like a well-lit throne. My uncle was a barber at West Point and gave the cadets their haircuts. I never liked those buzz cuts! This was a ritual. Sometimes it would interfere with my friends' plans for playing games or team sports, but that was the way it was. I never complained and followed the traditions of my family.

In a corner of the room was a gun locker with hunting shotguns. A stuffed pheasant sat on a side hutch. The pheasant was a worthy prize from a hunting trip of my grandfather's. My brother Lee ended up with that colorful pheasant, whose demise was the result of a curious house cat!

Sunday would be M&M day. Mass and Macaroni! After Mass it was time to walk to "Nanny Down's" for the traditional Sunday meal that was much more than just a meal. It was always an experience. My grandfather would meet us at the door. I can still see him. He always wore a white shirt. If it was hot out, he would roll up his sleeves and wear suspenders. El Productos were his favorite cigar. I can still remember that smell in the air and on his clothes when he would give all of us kids a kiss and at the same time squeeze a quarter into our hands.

Nanny Down, my Sicilian-speaking grandmother, made up names for us children. My oldest brother, Larry Junior, was called Junutz. She called my other brother Sal, Samutz. Brother Lee was referred to as Leedutz and sister Jacque was Jackiminetta. Margie was Margee and I was Georgi. To this day I still refer to them by these names. When I call and leave a voice mail message on their phones, I know mentioning these names brings warmth to their hearts and puts a smile on their faces.

My brothers and I all played Catholic Youth Organization (CYO) basketball. I grew into the game and enjoyed playing with my friends and classmates. John and I played CYO together under Coach Joe Alward. He was retired military from West Point. I remember him driving five of us in his car to Rockland County to play a team in Tomkins Cove. There was a little school located along Route 9W. Behind the school there was an outdoor basketball court up on a hill. We didn't bring a ball. The other team only had one old leather basketball. During the game the ball went out of bounds and rolled down the hill. A passing car hit the ball and deflated it. That was it. The game was over! We all piled into the car and left.

At that time, if girls could play, my sister Jacque probably would have made All Star. She did everything her brothers did, including hitting a punching bag we had hanging up in our garage. My brother Sal hung up the speed bag rack to one of the beams. When he hit that bag, the garage would shake. He taught me how to hit it. I enjoyed working out on the bag. We used to wear gloves with built-in weights. It was good for eye-hand coordination and timing. Jacque would even make that old garage shake!

There was a basketball rim without a net on a telephone pole on our street. That is where I learned to shoot and would practice till dark. When it was dinner time, Jacque would stand at the top of our steps and let out the loudest whistle ever heard. That whistle sound probably echoed up and down the Hudson Valley!

I continued to play basketball and run on the cross-country team in high school. John and I played for the JV coach Charlie Byrnes. During the end of our sophomore year, we moved up to varsity and played for Jerry Kaplan, a new coach who just moved into the area. I remember one day during practice we were told to go into the locker room. We listened to a radio announcement about JFK being shot. We were all silent. A few days later I remember having my grandparents and other relatives over at our house, eating. I watched on live TV when Ruby shot Oswald. I told my parents, and everyone in the house was in disbelief. That period of time felt very strange. It opened up a whole new live, violent chapter in our nation's history. A few years later on TV, you could see GIs killed in Vietnam coming home in body bags and the daily body count numbers posted on the news.

Overall, John and I had a very good career playing high school basketball. One of my most memorable high school experiences was when Coach Byrnes asked me if I wanted to go see the New York City Catholic high school championship game between Power Memorial High School and Archbishop Malloy High School. At seven feet tall, Lew Alcinder, now known as Kareem Abdul-Jabbar, played center for Power. Coach Byrnes's brother was the basketball coach at Cathedral High School. He met us at the game and made arrangements for us to sit right in front of the basket. I was in awe of Jabbar, and some of the other players were also very impressive. Jabbar went on to play in college at UCLA and professionally for Milwaukee and was one of the greatest in NBA history. Both John and I ended up going into the military!

While in high school I worked part time for James P. Grant, an

Irish immigrant who was a local bartender. He came to this country in the 1950s. At the age of sixteen, he arrived in New York Harbor, where he disembarked from the *Queen Mary* with only a suitcase. He looked for work and found out there was a job available at the Bear Mountain Inn. He ended up bartending there for over forty years. He became friends with my older brothers and sister. For a period of time, he lived in our house until he got settled. Early on weekend mornings, he and I would clean up the bars of two local establishments, the West Point Inn and the Trading Post Restaurant. Besides sweeping and mopping floors, I would go down into the cellars and stack beer bottles. I can still remember walking into the bar in the early morning to the stench of cigarettes, cigars, spilled beer, and whiskey. It was so nauseating that I never smoked cigarettes. I would ask myself how could people go out and enjoy themselves in this environment. I admit that over the years I have passed through some dives in and out of this country. That stale smell never fails to bring me back to those early years. Now that the laws have changed, there aren't many places remaining that you can smoke in. Just as the West Point Inn and the Trading Post went the way of a bulldozer, so did the local bars and their days of smoke-filled activities. Like smoking they, too, evaporated. Mr. Grant is still a very good friend. When I worked with him in my high school years, he would tell me over and over about the benefits of getting a good education and how he regretted not having a formal education himself. That might be so, but Jim did all right.

John and I also worked together part time at the Cadet Restaurant on West Point. During my senior year summer vacation, I worked at Bear Mountain State Park with my friends Jimmy LoRusso and Frankie DeBari. At the time my aunt Mary Graziano was in charge of the cafeteria on the ground floor of the Bear Mountain Inn. She was tough and had a reputation of yelling and screaming at the employees and sometimes even the customers! Whenever I walked past the cafeteria she would call me over, tell me to sit in the back, and make me something to eat. My boss there was Hale Adler, who was in charge of all the vending machines. I would help Hale fill the machines, fix them, clean them, and collect the money. I ended up working there until I entered the service.

I was very familiar with Bear Mountain. Uncle Lee would drive his wife, Mary, to work at Bear Mountain every day. When I was younger he would take us there to see the Golden Glove boxers. They would have their training and boxing matches there. Uncle Lee had been a boxer. I always remembered looking at his hands because his knuckles were disfigured. One time my nonno was there with us and the boxer Rocky Graziano showed up. A photo was taken of my nonno with his fist at Rocky's chin. That photo appeared on the back sports page of the *New York Daily News*. The article mentioned that they both have the same last name but no relation.

One evening I called my friend John. I had to work the following day but I also had my driving test scheduled in the morning in Newburgh. John already had his license and drove his mother's car. John's father had passed away early in life. John told me he would take the driver's test for me. At that time there was no photo license. We were both about the same height, weight, and description. I gave him the letter I received from the motor vehicle office. Later that day John came to see me on the job and told me he was sorry. What!! He said there was an elderly woman carrying some packages across the street and he just nicked her!! WHAT! He laughed. That was the type of relationship I had with John. My license came in the mail a few days later.

I could not do justice in describing some of the other locals. That would take another book! Like all small towns, everyone but everyone, and I mean everyone, knew everything about everything and everybody. You might think you could get away with something but you would be wrong, very wrong. And to top it off, just about everyone was related by marriage to someone in town!

My sister Margie passed away in November 1966 from cancer. She had two children, Teddi-Ann and Billie Jo. Once again my mother stepped up to do what she knew best and that was to help raise children.

These vignettes of growing up in a loving environment with traditions, habits, and rituals blanketed my feelings of security. It gave me a sense of not being afraid. It built confidence and allowed for hope, for positive expectations.

Repetition and structure build courage. I don't remember facing any fear when I was growing up. However, when my parents were growing up, they experienced a total transformation. Both being immigrants, they witnessed the sacrifice of change. While they believed in a better life here, they like most immigrants worried about what their lives would become in the new world. Living in an Italian neighborhood helped diffuse my parents' fears.

2

Military/College/
Post College

The Vietnam war was going strong when I graduated from high school. My high school friends Jim LoRusso, John Fitzpatrick, Ron Pizana, and Bob Gately were all going to join the Marine Corps. The military draft was in effect. I talked to my three brothers about it. My oldest brother Larry had graduated from West Point a few years earlier. Sal and Lee were still in the Army. They suggested I volunteer for the Air Force. I took their advice and joined up. I had been called for the draft and took my physical in lower Manhattan on Whitehall Street. It was easy to tell my parents I was going into the service because my other brothers had led the way. I think they expected that. We never spoke about attending a four-year college because I knew it wasn't financially feasible.

In January 1967, I entered the United States Air Force. It was only a few months after my sister Margie had passed away. Of course, my mom was still grieving but understood that I had to serve. After completing basic training at Lackland Air Force Base in Texas, I was selected to go into Security Police training. I was assigned to Davis-Monthan AFB, in Tucson, Arizona, to perform law enforcement and security duties.

While I was stationed in Tucson, I received a letter from Bob Gately. He was stationed at the Marine Corps Recruiting Depot (MCRD) in San Diego. We scheduled a weekend when I took a bus to visit him. I arrived in the early evening. I showed the military police my identification. They tracked down Gately. He was out training and not available until the next day. I told them I traveled from Tucson to spend the weekend with Gately. They offered me a bunk in the nearby cell. There were no prisoners in there. The next day I met up with Gately and we went to Tiajuana, Mexico. When I meet Marines I tell them I spent the night in the brig at MCRD! This turned out not to be the last time I would spent a night in a cell in the service.

In early 1968, Tech Sergeant Malcolm Keir called me into his office and told me that the Air Force Security Police was forming a special unit to go to Vietnam. After the TET offensive started in January of that year, the United States Air Force bases were being attacked. The U.S. wanted not only to deploy combat security teams to protect the bases but also to do search missions around the bases. It was a strictly voluntary force but it required successful completion of jungle training. I told him I would be interested and to submit my name. The Program was called Operation SafeSide.

A few weeks later I received my orders to go to Schofield Barracks, Hawaii. I was assigned to the 82nd Combat Security Police Squadron. This was the first training class of the newly formed unit. We were instructed by U.S. Army Rangers and Australian Rangers in various physical and weapons training. It was also mostly physical obstacle courses, water survival, and hand-to-hand combat training. Water survival was my biggest challenge because I did not know how to swim. We had to go up on a diving board with full gear and our M-16 rifle, where we would be blindfolded. We had to hold the rifle straight out in front of us. Then the instructor pushed us off the high board into the water. There were instructors at the edge of the pool with a hook to help those who lost their weapon or could not swim. I never lost my weapon but as soon as I hit that water, I was looking for that hook!

On maneuvers we would go into the mountains, passing sugar cane fields where we were told to cut off the canes and suck on them for energy. Once up in the mountains I could look out into the horizon of the Pacific and see surfers along the coast. What a contrast! The training was intense. I remember one evening on a weekend we were sitting around on our bunks back in the barracks. Someone had a portable radio, and we listened to the news of the recent assassination of Martin Luther King. Everyone was silent. This was the first news item we had heard in a month, and we did not know what was going on back on the mainland. Little did we know that a few months later, Robert Kennedy would also be assassinated.

While at Schofield I wrote home to my parents to tell them where I was, what I was doing, and that I was on my way to Vietnam. Later, I would realize that was a big mistake, one I still regret.

We were all in full combat gear with our M-16s, sitting on the tarmac waiting to load up into a cargo plane. It was raining and we had our ponchos on. This was now April 1968 and we were going to be deployed to Phan Rang, Vietnam. We were going to relieve the 1st Brigade, 101st Airborne Division. They were providing security for the base. Later, two more classes were completed at Schofield and then the school was transferred to Ft. Campbell, Kentucky.

While I was sitting on the tarmac, I realized that I would be finally going to a war zone that I had heard so much about from friends and others who were there and had written to me. In the distance I could see an open-air jeep driving slowly along the tarmac. Our captain was standing up, cupping his hands around his mouth, calling out something. The guy next to me said, "I think he is calling your name." When the jeep got closer, I could hear the captain calling, "DAPRA!" I stood up and the jeep stopped near me. The captain asked me my name. I told him and he said, "Get in." I threw my gear in the back of the jeep and we drove back to Headquarters, where the captain told me to report to the colonel, the commandant of the school. I went in and reported to Colonel Purdy, who was sitting behind his desk, looking through a folder. He said to me, "Are you from Highland Falls, New York?"

"Yes, sir."

"Do you know Waldo Wood?"

"Yes, sir. He was the football coach and is the athletic director at the high school."

He replied, "I am from Monroe, and I played against him in football and baseball. He is the toughest SOB I ever met. Do you know what is going on back home with your mother?"

"No, sir."

The colonel picked up the folder and took out a letter. He said, "I have a letter here from your parish priest, Father Thomas McDonald, and Assemblyman Ben Gilman. They are asking that you not go to Vietnam because your mother had a nervous breakdown when she heard you were going. They say that your mother lost a daughter to cancer a few years ago and she is helping raise two infants. Then her mother passed away last year and she is also taking care of her elderly father. Is this true?"

"Yes, sir."

"Well, son, I suggest you take leave, go back home, and be with your mother for a while. The war will still be going on. I know you volunteered but after you return from your leave and you go back to your base, you can reapply again if you want. You have completed all the training and have the certificate of completion, correct?"

"Yes, sir." I saluted him and he wished me well. The next day I flew back to the States and never heard from or saw the other guys I completed that school with. There was one other guy I flew back to the States with. He had developed a skin condition in the mountains of Hawaii. His face was peeling off. He told me he was going to be discharged from the service because he caught some fungus and would never be able to go into the sun again.

I went home for a week. Of course, my mother was very excited to see me home and I spent the whole time with my parents. My mother was better than I expected. I told her I had to return to Arizona but not to worry because I would be in the States. My oldest brother Larry was still in the service with his family. Sal and Lee were out of the Army at that time and living near my parents. My sister Jacque was married and also living in town, so my mother had a support system. I never spoke to anyone about what that whole episode was about with my mother. Even when I was home and went to church and saw Father McDonald, he never said a word to me about going to Vietnam. I thought the whole episode was a little strange.

When I returned to Davis-Monthan AFB in Tucson, I talked to TSGT Keir and advised him of the situation and my conversation with the colonel in Hawaii. He asked me if I wanted to submit my name again to volunteer for Vietnam. I told him yes. Keir showed me the paperwork he submitted on my behalf. About six months went by and I hadn't heard from anyone.

Shortly thereafter TSGT Keir advised me that they were looking for someone to go on a temporary duty assignment (TDY) for thirty days to Fort Huachuca in southern Arizona near the Mexican border. I said yes. I would be assigned to the Army's Military Police unit at the base. Before I went into the service I had been told never to volunteer for anything. So, here I was volunteering for another assignment after the failed Vietnam episode. This one didn't turn out so well either.

I found military life to be like a separate closed society. But it was also a melting pot. The guys I met in the service were Yankees from up North; good old boys from the South; cowboys, Texans, and a racial mix that didn't get along. They were mostly all young and trained to fight. And fight they did. I was involved in more fist-fights and breaking up fights than at any other time in my life. I didn't know if it was the 100-plus-degree heat or the firewater they drank. Or it could have been we were not too far from Tombstone and the OK Corral. I saw a military policeman shoot another soldier who was trying to escape from an arrest. The MP pulled out his .45 and shot the guy in the lower back. It blew out the guy's guts. My TDY tour was up so I never heard what happened to that MP.

When I returned to my base I tried to call Col. Purdy in Hawaii and was told he retired. In the meantime, I was promoted to sergeant and my new duties were desk sergeant for operations. I would ask TSgt Keir about my status and to check on it and he would tell me he hadn't heard anything. A few months later I was transferred into Security Police Investigations. I would work cases with career Staff Sergeant Nelson Harrison, who was from the inner city of Newark, New Jersey. He and I got along well. There was another career staff sergeant, Bill Baker who was from Harlem. He was in charge of the barracks. He would always tell me, "Dap, you got to buy land out here!"

I told him, "Why would I want to buy dirt?" I would tell him I would if I had his money. He owned a small bar with an apartment above that he rented out. It was in a rundown section in downtown Tucson. Years later I would say to myself that Baker was smarter than I thought at the time.

After another six months or so went by, a friend of mine named Jack Perrault, who worked in Personnel, called me to say he received a notice that I had orders. He asked me to come over to his office. I arrived and he said, "You are going to Korea!" I said, "KOREA!" He told me I had thirty days to report. I asked him who else knew about this and he said no one yet. He hadn't logged in the orders. I knew he was getting short so I asked him how much time he had left before his enlistment was up. He told me that in ten days he would be back in Templeton, Mass. I said, "Let me see those orders." I took the orders from him, ripped them up, and threw them in the trash can. I told him, "You will be back home," and not to worry. He said, "You are crazy!"

Even though it was very uncharacteristic of this good little altar boy, I realized I had a little over a year left on my enlistment in the service. I figured the Air Force would not be sending me to Vietnam even after I volunteered twice and went through some very difficult training. I didn't expect a tour somewhere else overseas. That's military life. Also, I had just started applying to the University of Arizona and establishing residency in order to pay in-state tuition. My plan was to go to school there after my enlistment was up. Part of my frustration with the assignment was it did not sound logical. I was surprised and it caught me off guard. It did not follow my personal plans. Then I remembered, I WAS IN THE MILITARY! This was my first bad taste of conflict with the system. But I got over it and waited to see if they would hammer me before my time was up.

A few months passed and I hadn't heard from anyone. This was now early 1970. My enlistment would be up in January of 1971. I thought I was getting closer to be home free until...

One day I was in my office and Capt. Walker called me into his office right down the hall. He said, "What the hell are you doing?"

"About what?"

"You are supposed to be in Korea! I received a teletype from Headquarters. They are looking for you. They think you deserted!"

I played stupid. "You know I have been right here. I haven't gone anywhere. You promoted me and I got moved into this new position here."

He said, "I have to make some phone calls and I will talk to you later." About an hour later he came into my office with SSgt Harrison. By coincidence I had just received a phone call from Col. Malkemes, U.S. Army. It was perfect timing. I dated his daughter Marilyn in high school when their family was stationed at West Point. Col. Malkemes hadn't spoken to me in a few years and was just following up to see how I was doing in the service. The last time I had seen him we had driven Marilyn to the airport for her flight to Radford, Virginia, where she went to college. Capt. Walker and SSgt Harrison sat down in my office while I was on the phone. The sun was shining in through the window and was hitting right where Harrison was sitting. When I looked at the captain I could see Harrison ablaze like an Arizona sunrise.

I responded to Col. Malkemes with "Yes, Colonel. Yes, Colonel. Everything is fine, Colonel." I then put him on speakerphone and said, "Colonel, I am sorry I have to cut you short but I have some visitors in my office and have to go." Capt. Walker could hear him say, "Okay, George, good talking to you. If you need anything or if I could be any help just give me a call." I said, "Thank you, Colonel. I will," and then I hung up the phone.

Capt. Walker said, "Who the hell was that?"

I said, "Just a friend of mine in Headquarters."

The captain was dumbfounded. I glanced at Harrison, who had the biggest smile on his face that I had ever seen!

Capt. Walker said, "I don't know what Headquarters is going to do, but I suggest you talk to an attorney in the Staff Judge Advocate's Office."

I said, "Okay." They got up and left the room.

So, that is what I did. The attorney I saw from the Staff Judge Advocate's Office advised me that I would be getting an Article 15 for missing an overseas assignment. I was reduced in rank from an E4 to an E3. An Article 15 of the Uniform Code of Military Justice is a non-judicial punishment. This means that it is not considered a judicial proceeding like a court martial. It permits the commander to resolve minor misconduct. I signed some papers and went back to work.

Capt. Walker informed me that they were making plans for me to leave the following week. That week he came into my office again with Harrison and said, "Headquarters wants to make sure you are going to get on the plane this time; so they are putting you in a bunk in the cell to sleep. And you will be escorted to the plane." I didn't have a problem with it. I asked, "Am I under arrest?" He and Harrison said, "No." It was war time and they didn't want me to get charged with desertion in case something happened. I told them I was going to Korea. Capt. Walker then said to me, "Make sure you clean out your room in the barracks." Harrison looked at me and winked. He knew I had an apartment off base with some other guys from the barracks. We all worked different shifts and would hang out in the apartment on our time off with our girlfriends. My room-mate in the barracks was Mike Dietrich from Fargo, North Dakota. He was one of the guys who stayed in the apartment. Also living in the apartment was Jim Koch.

In August of 2016, I received a pleasant and very surprising phone call. Elaine answered the phone. I was out working in the garden. She came out and said, "Someone from Texas by the name of Jim is on the phone and he is asking for Georgie." I got on the phone and it was Jim Koch! He had tracked me down. He told me he had retired from the Tucson Police Department and was a police chief in New Mexico. He was at a recent police reunion with his wife, Sharon, who asked him if he ever heard from the guys he was in the service with. So he started looking. We had a very long, good conversation about our lives since the military. We also spoke about living in that apartment and I remembered Sharon, who lived in the same complex. We exchanged contact information and keep in touch. In 2017, Elaine and I while out in Texas visiting relatives, met Jim and Sharon for an enjoyable lunch.

We rarely lived in the barracks room but it was kept in perfect condition for unannounced inspections. So, I had to also clean out my personal effects from the apartment. And I had to get rid of my car. I had a 1963 Triumph Spitfire convertible, light blue. It was great for riding in the evenings in the desert air. On short notice I ended up selling it for half of what it was worth.

During this whole episode I never wrote or called my brothers Larry, Sal, or Lee. Neither did I call my parents or tell any of my friends. The only people who knew about this were the military personnel around me at the time. I felt embarrassed. As far as I knew, my brothers had very good records in the service. To this day I don't think they, my other family members, or friends knew of my Article 15. Never did anyone in my family contact me with their plan of going to the local politician and Father McDonald for letters to send to the Air Force. They had no idea I had volunteered. Shortly before I was to leave for Korea, I called my mother to tell her I was going overseas and it was not Vietnam. I told her it would be a better assignment, I would write home, and not to worry because I would be out of the service within the year. She was fine with that.

The evening before I was to leave, I packed my bags. In my bag I threw in a copy of the book The Godfather that I recently bought and just started reading. I brought my bags to the office. Capt. Walker was there and gave me my personnel file with instructions to present it to my new duty station. Harrison showed up to wish me well. I thanked them all. The desk sergeant on operations was Roy Leighton from Maine. There were no prisoners in the cells behind operations. He had put chocolates on the bunk for me! I ended up talking to him and the night shift most of the night. They went out and got me food. Early the next morning they took me to the airport. I had a connecting flight in Los Angeles. When I was in the terminal, I went into the men's room and opened up my personnel file. I ripped out all the derogatory information about my Article 15 and threw it into the trash can!

When I arrived at my new duty station, 6171st Security Police Squadron, Kwang Ju Air Base, Korea, no one questioned me about missing my original reporting date. I was just the new guy reporting for duty. Kwang Ju was a small joint Air Force and Korean base with a detachment of U.S. F-16 fighter jets. My duties were base and village patrols. There was only a small detachment of Americans on the base. The whole country was under an 11 PM curfew. No one was allowed out on the streets after curfew, and that was one of the reasons for our patrols in the area. One of our other patrols was to check the two "nightclubs" in the village. Whenever any Korean girls went into the club, they would have to have medical cards with them, which they would leave with the hostess at the door who would post them on a board. We would randomly go into the clubs to make sure that policy was followed. Once a week the girls had to report to the base for medical exams.

My staff sergeant for the night shift would park his jeep outside a "hooch" in the village where he lived with a Korean woman during the day. He told us if we ever needed him, to call him on the radio. One of the reasons he frequented the house at night is that the American servicemen who lived in the village and worked the day shift would leave in the morning and walk to the base for work. The servicemen who worked nights would get off in the morning and go to the same hooch that the day shift guy was just leaving! My staff sergeant wanted to make sure no one else was sleeping in the same house. Some servicemen would bring the locals cigarettes and liquor from the base.

I had a good working relationship with our interpreter, Mr. Chun Pong Chae. He was from Kwang Ju City. He would invite me to his home, where he conducted weekly English language classes for some of his friends and neighbors. I would go and help him with questions from his students. When Thanksgiving approached, he asked if I would be willing to get a few of my other American servicemen to adopt an orphan for Thanksgiving Day and bring them to the base for dinner. I made arrangements with my commander and got some other guys to join me. We brought a group of orphans on base for a special Thanksgiving Day dinner and gave them doggie bags to take with them. I exchanged letters and Christmas cards with Mr. Chae for many years after I left Korea.

My tour and enlistment were coming to an end in January of 1971. My commander asked if I wanted to go to the Bob Hope USO Show for Christmas. Hope would be appearing near the DMZ. I told him I was leaving in a few weeks and suggested that he let some of the other guys who had more time left in country to go instead.

The main gate to the base always had one Korean MP on duty and one American. I only had a few days left in the country and I was assigned to fill in and relieve the main gate for breaks. One afternoon I drove a jeep out to the gate to relieve the MP, a guy from Missouri. He was upset about something, and the Korean MP was on the phone to his office, yelling and screaming in Korean. I had walked into a hornets' nest!

I asked the guy what was going on and he wouldn't say anything. Then the Korean hung up the phone. I started taking care of business out on the road at the entrance by checking people and vehicles coming on the base. The next thing I heard was a BANG! The American shot the Korean! The bullet entered the Korean's mouth and exited his cheek. He was on the floor of the gate house, rolling around and screaming. The American called our office. Everyone responded, including the Korean and American bosses. The Korean was taken to the base hospital. That night the American was out of the country and on a flight to Okinawa. The Korean's were furious and wanted to prosecute the American for attempted murder. I never heard why the American shot the Korean. My tour was up shortly thereafter.

I was honorably discharged on January of 1971 at McCord Air Force Base, Spokane, Washington. I had made plans to go to Cambria, California, and visit my old high school friend Ron Pizana. Ron, who was in the Marines, was badly wounded in Vietnam. The day I got discharged I still had my uniform on. I was going to fly to San Francisco, get a hotel room for the night, change into civilian clothes, and get a bus the next day to Cambria. After I arrived in San Francisco, I tried to check into a Hyatt Hotel while in uniform. I was ignored and then told there were no rooms. I went to another chain hotel and was told the same story and denied a room. The third hotel I went into, I was ignored altogether. Finally, I went to a fleabag hotel near the bus depot. The Vietnam war was still on and there was plenty of anti-war fever in California. That was the last day I wore my military uniform.

The next day I took a bus to Cambria and visited Pizana. It was good to see him but he was in a bad place physically and mentally. He was living with some other former Marines from Vietnam and there were a lot of drugs around. I left the next day. After I got out of the service, the only friend from high school who I never heard from again was Bob Gately. In Vietnam John, Jimmy, and Ron all were wounded. All received Purple Hearts. John and Ron also received Bronze Stars and all are on VA disability.

After that trip, I traveled back to Tucson, where I had been stationed before Korea. For a while I was staying with Ron DeMichele, an old friend from New York who was at the university. Ron had a room at the College Inn. I stayed with him until I could get settled. In the spring of 1971, I enrolled in the University of Arizona. Under the GI Bill I was awarded $175 a month. I am very thankful for the generosity of my brother Lee, who lent me money to get settled. My student loans from Valley National Bank paid for my tuition. I went straight through college, going to summer school each year. While on campus one day I met David Lee, one of the security policemen I had been stationed with at Davis-Monthan Air Force Base. He was excited to see me again. He couldn't believe we met. He told me they were still talking about my missed assignment and sleeping in the cell. We got together a few times after that and even double-dated once.

While I was enrolled at the university, I used to take some of my breaks in Mexico. In 1972 and 1973, I spent spring break in Mexico City. One year I flew to Mexico City via Dallas. Another year I went to Mexico City by bus. It took about two days or so and was quite interesting. Not only did I meet some locals but I also got to know some caged chickens! At one of our scheduled stops in a dusty little village, I strayed into an open-air cantina for a beer. Luckily, a passenger on the bus saw me go there. He came running to get me because the bus was leaving. The bus driver had announced in Spanish that we would only be there for five minutes. I thought he said twenty-five minutes!

In both of my trips to Mexico City, I stayed in a small clean hotel called Hotel de las Americas off Paseo de la Reforma, the main boulevard in Mexico City. The rate was five dollars a night. It was not far from the Zona Rosa, which was a good tourist area near the American Embassy. I enjoyed visiting Chapultepec Park, where there were museums, beautiful fountains, and a castle. I also took a bus to Cuernavaca, a lovely town not too far away. One of the reasons I had chosen to visit Mexico City was on the recommendation of a student friend by the name of Carmen Arce. She lived in the apartment complex I was residing in on Euclid Avenue in Tucson. Carmen was from San Jose, Costa Rica, and told me her father was a diplomat. She visited Mexico City numerous times, knew the city well, and gave me reliable information.

One day walking down La Reforma in Mexico City, I met a girl by the name of Cecilia Bellacetin, who worked for an insurance company. She showed me around Mexico City and we enjoyed each other's company. She invited me to come out to her parents' house for Easter. She gave me her address in the Col. San Pedro el Chico neighborhood and told me how to take two different buses to get there by mid-afternoon. She also told me to bring a change of clothes. I was excited and intrigued!

After I went to a nearby church for Easter services, I followed her directions to the neighborhood. The bus stop was a few blocks from the house. I walked down the street carrying a small overnight bag, looking for the number of her house. When I arrived at the door, I knocked. There was no answer. I waited a few minutes then knocked again. No answer. Then I could hear distant giggling. I looked around but there was no one around. The street was quiet. I stood there for a second and was just about to knock again when I got soaked by a torrent of water from the roof! Cecilia and her sisters were up on the roof with buckets of water. They were laughing. This was why I had to bring a change of clothes! According to Cecilia, this was a family tradition for Easter and so that any new friends who visited their house would be clean. I told them I didn't need a change of clothes, I needed an umbrella. I went into the house and her parents welcomed me. I changed and they had a huge meal prepared. Her parents could not speak English. Cecilia interpreted. Her father asked me my heritage and I told him about my mother being born in Sicily and my father from Northern Italy. He beamed and got up and walked into his bedroom. He came out with a book, *El Padrino*—the Mexican edition of *The Godfather*. He told me how he admired the Corleone family. He owned a gun store in Mexico City. What a small world—*The Godfather* was already in Mexico!.

During another semester break I traveled to New York to visit my parents. While home my brother Lee was very generous and let me use his Corvette. Both Sal and Lee were boilermakers with the Local 5 Union in New York. My mother told me for the first time that we had relatives in the Phoenix area, Phil and Theresa Sollomi, who was Aunt Jemma's daughter—remember? My parents' honeymoon was to take Aunt Jemma home to Cleveland.

Upon my return to Arizona, I contacted them and spent many weekends with them and their children. During one of my visits, I asked how they ended up in Arizona. Phil explained that in the 1950s they had lived in Kansas City above a little Italian restaurant they operated. He started making his own salad dressing at the request of his regular customers, and he began to bottle and sell it. The demand was so great that he set up the basement of the restaurant as a little factory where he was bottling jars of salad dressing. He then set up a distribution network around the country. One day, Lipton Soup contacted him and wanted to buy the business. Phil went to their headquarters in northern New Jersey with his attorneys to sell the business. He sat in a large conference room with all the attorneys from the company and his private attorneys. On the table he noticed a thick folder in front of Lipton's attorneys that was never opened. A few days after the sale, Phil was talking to one of his attorneys about the sale. He wanted to know what was in that thick folder that sat so ominously on the table. One of the attorneys told Phil that Lipton had conducted a background check on him because he was Italian, to make sure that he was legit and not connected to any organized crime group. Phil was upset and told his attorney that if he had known that before the sale, he wouldn't have done business with Lipton. He said, "I hope they found out I graduated from Ohio State University!" The name of that little restaurant they lived above and operated was the Wishbone. Part of the deal was Lipton had to keep the name. After the sale, Phil and Theresa moved to Phoenix, where he invested in real estate and other businesses. Over the years I had some very good conversations with Phil about his charitable works for the Catholic church and the community.

Starting college after military life was a refreshing experience. I enrolled in some night classes at the University of Arizona. I took a class in Italian and became friends with the instructor, Mario Erante, who used to have me over his house for dinner with his family. They were originally from Long Island. This was right around the time that my friend Ron finished school and returned to New York. I was searching for an apartment and answered an ad in the university newspaper to share an apartment. I met the occupants, Roger Brown, a U of A graduate who was working for a local hospital, and Jim Glenney and his girlfriend Darcy Twyman. Jim was a graduate of Williams College and was working on his master's degree. He was from Texas, and Darcy was from Michigan and a member of the Kappa Kappa Gamma sorority. The apartment on Euclid Avenue was walking distance to school, and the apartment complex had a pool. It was affordable. They made arrangements for me to meet them. They were all good people. Actually, they interviewed me like it was for employment. I understood and passed. We all got along very well. I found it interesting because it was like meeting new people when I was in the military. You were sharing space with others and had to learn to get along with people from various backgrounds. After we got to know one another, they told me they were suspicious of me because I was an Italian from New York! At this time in Tucson, there were plenty of news stories about Joe Bonanno, the New York crime boss who owned a modest house in Tucson. There was an incident in the news when someone threw an explosive device at his house. Of course, other stories came out saying the FBI did it to start a war within the family. But more about that story later.

One of my other classes was in a large lecture hall. One day leaving a class, I recognized a guy sitting in one of the chairs in a nearby classroom. It was Paul Formentini. I knew Paul from the College Inn, where he lived and was introduced to me by my friend Ron. Paul had his golf putter with him and was using it to help himself to get up. Other students were just walking past him. I stopped and asked if he needed help. He said, "Yes, but you have to pick me up under my arms." After I helped him up and his back was straight, he was able to walk. Paul was from Illinois. In his senior year of high school, he started to have problems walking. He was diagnosed with a muscle disorder. On his own he moved to Arizona. I took Paul to see the new movie *The Godfather* at a local theater. After the movie we discussed our Italian roots. Paul had told me his life expectancy was only in the thirties because of his medical condition. Today, he is still living in Tucson and is married with two daughters.

In December 1974, I graduated with a degree in Public Administration. When I left Arizona I gave Paul a bottle of Italian wine. I told him he couldn't drink it until I came back and we were both retired. On my way back to New York, I flew to Houston, Texas, for a few days to visit Jim and Darcy. They, too, had finished school and returned to Houston. One evening Jim took me to a very good Italian restaurant in Houston called Tony's. It was a pleasant dinner and I got to meet Jim's family.

When I returned to New York City in the mid-1970s, it was going through tough times. The whole country was in a recession. But in the city, it felt like it was going down the sewer. In the summers there were garbage strikes and power blackouts. There was looting. The city stunk. The crime rate was off the charts. In 1975, the city was broke and laying off police officers. On the front page of the *New York Daily News*, President Ford's famous quote roared: "Ford to city-Drop Dead." There were few jobs available. I flooded my resume to companies and the government. I took a political class at The New School that included a visit to Washington, D.C. and Congress. I knocked on doors of representatives and many government agencies looking for work. All to no avail.

One day I saw an ad in the *New York Times* for a security/house detective at the Plaza Hotel. I applied for the job and was hired. The chief of security was Major Savino, a barrel-chested former Marine who kept his rank with his name. I don't think I ever knew his real first name. He ran a tight ship; it was shift work, which I didn't mind. Possibly the most famous hotel in New York and world-renowned, the Plaza was built in 1907. The landmark became famous thanks to the numerous movies that were filmed there. The employees, permanent residents, and celebrity guests created a revolving door of mysterious characters with stories to tell and secrets to keep. At times it felt like the small town Peyton Place. It felt like the backdrop of a Broadway set, with a different cast of characters performing each night. The Persian Room nightclub, the Edwardian Room, Oak Room, Oak Bar, Palm Court, Oyster Bar, and Trader Vic's were all operating and bustling. There were nights when the hotel was packed with guests, tourists, and visitors. Other times it was quiet and sedate. Of course, the Plaza's prestigious clientele created the perfect environment for hustlers, thieves, prostitutes, and pickpockets. Some were high-class con artists and some were professional hotel thieves who checked into the hotel as a guest. It was against the law to be above the hotel lobby unless you were a registered guest. That was considered criminal trespassing. Those are the charges we would bring against prostitutes we would arrest arriving or after visiting clients.

My favorite location was the Oak Bar with the huge mural paintings by Everett Shinn depicting scenes of New York around the outside of the hotel in the early 1900s. The paintings were from the 1940s.

Up until 1970, women were not allowed in the Oak Bar. There were telephones on each table, and the captains of industry—bankers, lawyers, and politicians—could call other tables to conduct business. Some late nights I would walk into the room just to soak up the atmosphere that was alive with chatter and laughter and history. At the round table in the corner on the left near the entrance to the Oak Room, Truman Capote would hold court with James Baldwin and other artists, poets, writers, and actors. It was a long road from cleaning local bars in high school to the Oak Bar! Years later I read that the FBI's Counter Intelligence Unit had Baldwin under surveillance during the 1960s and '70s.

One of the bartenders, Sammy, would fill me in on all the activity going on in the room. Sammy was still working there up until the change of ownership of the hotel in 2007. The exterior of the historic hotel is protected from change. However, now it is part hotel and condos. Most of those multimillion-dollar condos are owned by foreigners and are only occasionally occupied by the owners during the year. All the original restaurants and bars are closed. There is a new food court and shops on the lower level. The sophistication and drama of the Plaza's past have eroded with time.

One night I received a call from the front desk that a guest complained of someone yelling for help. I proceeded up to the floor and could hear a male voice calling out. I knocked and entered the room with my pass key. I could hear a voice coming from the bathroom. I walked in and there was a naked man on the floor tied up by belts and wet towels to the plumbing under the sink. He was squirming and crying. His body was covered with red welts. I untied him. He told me he thought he was going to die. He was a Swiss banker who met a male prostitute in the Oak Bar. The prostitute relieved the banker of his jewelry, wallet, cash, and travelers checks.

A few weeks later there was another early morning call, this time from the hotel operator. The dairy deliveryman said there was something at the 58th Street entrance. When I arrived, he was standing in the foyer of the entrance. He was disturbed and said very somberly, "You aren't going to believe this. Look out there." I walked out on the sidewalk and blinked a few times, trying to distinguish between the sleep in my eyes and the fog on the street in the early morning. There sat a perfectly upright human torso planted in the middle of the sidewalk. The head was sloped down toward the pavement, and the arms were relaxed on either side as if the cement had formed around it.

I looked up and down the street. There was no one around. It was around 5 AM. I got up close to the torso and walked around it. It was a male body cut perfectly in half. I told the deliveryman and some other hotel workers at the doorway to have the operator call NYPD. Not far from the torso was a construction Dumpster at the curb. As I looked up at the Dumpster, it took a moment to register, but there on the edge was a pair of pants with the bottom of a body. It was starting to drizzle and I asked one of the hotel workers to go and get a sheet. I covered the torso. NYPD showed up and then some homicide detectives. It started getting light out; people started coming to work, so NYPD closed down the sidewalk. One of the detectives climbed up to the top of the Dumpster and went through the pants and retrieved a wallet. It turned out that the man was a guest of the hotel, staying on one of the upper floors. We went up to his room. I unlocked and slowly opened the door. It was a very eerie scene right out of a Hitchcock movie. There was a woman asleep in the bed, lying on her back with a sheet up to her chin, and a large open window next to the bed that had sheer curtains blowing out of the window. One of the homicide detectives took out a pen flashlight and got close to the woman and shined it in her eyes. She jumped up screaming and went into shock. After she calmed down, she told us that she and her husband had been out on the town and had had too much to drink. They were with other friends who were also guests in the hotel. There was some vomit on the floor and on the windowsill, which was very low. The husband must have vomited out the window and fallen out. The Dumpster was below. His body had hit the edge and it had cut him completely in half. Not a sight that is easily forgotten! I quickly learned that in this type of job, anything could and did happen. Nothing really prepared me for that as much as this incident did.

Most of the other guys I worked with were looking for other law enforcement jobs. We became good friends, and I still keep in touch with some, but mostly with Joe Montagna, who was a former police officer in Key West, Florida. Ron Shedd had joined but resigned from the ATF. Bart Scheinder became a U.S. Border Patrol agent. Bruce Koscoff went to work for the Port Authority Police. Mike Fallon became an FBI agent. Larry Frost married Nancy Gorden, a Plaza employee, and he became a well-known private investigator working for some of NYC's high-profile criminal defense attorneys. Montagna called me in 2013 to tell me Larry passed away months earlier. I was shocked. I hadn't seen or talked to Larry in a few years.

Working at the Plaza opened my eyes to a different world, but it reinforced my desire to build up my resume and seek government law enforcement positions just like my coworkers were. Meeting other people who had similar backgrounds made me realize that my own search for a career would be better served if I continued to pursue law enforcement positions because I had the military police experience and a college degree.

Over the years, I have met numerous people who would never guess my occupation. People who knew me would ask, "How did you get into law enforcement?"

My answer was always the same: military, college, and waking up in the Plaza Hotel.

"Oh, you stayed in the Plaza!" Yes, I have and it was probably one of the most enjoyable jobs I ever had.

Recently, my friend Montagna sent me an email. He had stopped by the Plaza and taken some photos of the changes at the old hotel and included the photos in his email. The hotel lobby is now in the area that used to be the Persian Room. Now there is a bar in the middle of the Palm Court. Eloise is still hanging on the 58th Street side. On the 59th Street side there is a large wall-sized photo of Frank Sinatra and Mia Farrow wearing masks, leaving one of the famous parties at the Plaza. In his email Joe quoted one of Elvis' songs about memories. We were able to get together and walk around the hotel and reminisce.

Back in the late 1970s, Joe left the Plaza and went to work for Loews Hotel Corporation as a security supervisor. He called me one day back then to ask if I would be interested in a night supervisor's job at Loews. At the time I was taking all the federal law enforcement exams for a federal job while still at the Plaza, but nothing had panned out yet.

I accepted the night supervisor's job with Loews. Even though I enjoyed working at the Plaza, this new position paid more and had better benefits. The Tisch family controlled Loew's Corporation, which managed five midtown hotels including the Regency (where one of the Tisch families lived), the Drake, the Warwick, the Summit, and the Ramada and Howard Johnson on the West Side. Each hotel had its own chief of security. I would check with them and be available out of Loews' corporate offices at 666 Fifth Avenue if there were any issues during the night and then I would report in the morning to Loews' director of security, who at the time was Harry Smith, a retired NYPD lieutenant. I was authorized to eat at any of the restaurants in any of the hotels and just sign the check. Some mornings I would alternate having breakfast with the different front office managers.

One morning I was walking to the Warwick Hotel on 54th Street to meet the manager for breakfast when I noticed a man with a short black leather jacket walking a small white dog outside the hotel. I entered the hotel, went into the front office, and met the manager. He asked me if I saw the guy outside and I told him I did. He informed me that it was Meyer Lansky, the infamous gangster and mob money man. He said Lansky checked into the hotel with his wife and dog under an alias when he was in the city. We talked for a while and then he told me he had to finish something and would meet me in the restaurant in a few minutes.

When I entered the restaurant, I saw Lansky seated by himself. The waiter sat me at the table next to Lansky, who was looking at the menu. He looked up and saw me and looked at my briefcase. He got up and told the waiter he changed his mind and wasn't hungry. When the manager showed up, I relayed the story to him. He said I wasn't even a real "copper" and Lansky could smell me. We enjoyed our breakfast and had a few laughs.

Loews was a good company to work for. In my pay envelope there would be show tickets or coupons for various activities around the city.

At the time I was in a serious relationship with Elaine, who was originally from Brooklyn. We knew one another from town. I knew this night shift work would not be good for a serious relationship. In 1976, I had applied for and secured a position with the NY State Tax Commission as a revenue agent. My territory was Orange County. Elaine had been hired as a teacher in the Highland Falls School District, also in Orange County. I proposed to Elaine and we planned to marry in 1977.

My supervisor in White Plains was Mike Campagna. One day he gave me a case on Gene Leone, the owner of Mamma Leone's restaurant in the city. I made an appointment to meet with Mr. Leone at his farm in Central Valley. After we completed business he showed me around the farm and pointed out the many acres he donated to West Point for training. He also showed me photos of his son with General MacArthur and photos of President Eisenhower at the farm. Mr. Leone was made an honorary member of the famous West Point Class of 1915. He asked me if I was married and I told him I would be getting married the following week. He called to his wife Mary to bring him a copy of his cookbook. President Eisenhower wrote the foreword in the book. They both proudly autographed the book and wrote, "For the Dapras, all good wishes for a happy married life. Auguri, Salute e Pace." He was a real gentleman. He told me the story of how his mother, Luisa, was the real mother Leone who opened the restaurant in 1906. At one point they were serving four thousand meals a day. In 1959, the restaurant was sold to Restaurant Associates, which was the same company that also managed the Bear Mountain Inn for a period of time. In 1994, Mamma Leone's closed for good. We still have the book and use some of his recipes.

Elaine and I married the following week and honeymooned in Acapulco, Mexico. For our first wedding anniversary, we decided to visit my brother Larry and his family, who were stationed in Vicenza,

Italy. Vicenza was a few hours south of the Trentino region. After my father's mother passed away in 1955, my father failed to continue to communicate with his relatives back in Trentino. My brother wanted us to come over and to visit my father's hometown of Panchia. Larry hadn't been able to visit yet. We only had the name of Aunt Elena but didn't know if she was still alive. We went over in July 1978. Larry, his daughter Suzanne, Elaine, and I drove up into the mountains to find Panchia and search for Elena.

When the Roman Empire fell apart and the barbarian invasions started, the valley became a shelter for fugitives desperately looking for a hidden and inaccessible haven. Since 1004, Trentino had been a principality of the Holy Roman Empire of Germany and only lost its sovereignty in 1803 with the abrogation of the Holy Roman Empire and its principalities. During the ten years from 1803 to 1813, Trentino experienced Austrian, Bavarian, and French occupations. Occupied by Austria again in 1813, it was annexed to the Austrian State in 1815. It was only after the Second World War that autonomy could be achieved. The Degasperi-Gruber Pact between Italy and Austria in 1946 granted a special autonomy to the province.[1]

After driving the mountain roads and into the valley, we stopped and asked people in the village of Panchia where Elena lived. We walked over hills like in *The Sound of Music* and found Elena's alpine-style house on a hill. We knocked on her door. After a short wait, a stout, sturdy, elderly woman wearing an apron and scarf answered the door. My brother Larry introduced us. She looked at all of us in amazement. Happily she invited us in. She was excited that we found her. She poured us all a glass of Lambrusco red wine to celebrate. However, she was a little upset that we were not fluent in Italian and no one had written to her in years. She pulled out photos of us as young kids that our grandmother had sent to her. She was elderly and not in good health. She used a cane in each hand to get around.

Elena was the last of my father's living relatives. We took photos with her and then went to explore the village. We went to the town hall, where we met the mayor, who spoke German and Italian. He was thrilled that we visited. He proudly escorted us into a room where he brought out a large ledger showing us our family tree going back to the 1700s. The last entry under our father's name was blank. So he instructed us to list the sons of our father. Larry entered the four boys' names into the ledger to keep the family tree going. The mayor wanted to know why our grandfather left the area with his family. We did not know why. This area did not have a large migration as compared to Southern Italy. The mayor proudly made copies of the ledger and gave them to us. I wanted to pay him for these services but he refused to take any money. We proceeded to the cemetery, where we took photos. All the plots have photos of the deceased on the gravestones. Another person we met showed us a stone aqueduct that our grandfather had built.

Our only unfortunate experience was when we went to the local church. It was locked, so we knocked on the rectory door. We had been waiting outside for a while when we heard a noise on the second-floor balcony overlooking the driveway where we were standing. The local priest came to the balcony and looked down at us. He had a napkin around his neck. It was lunchtime, which we didn't realize, and that was our mistake! We told him where we were from and wanted to look at the church and to see if there were any family records. He asked us which way we drove into the valley, from the mountain road or the autostrada. We told him the autostrada. He took his napkin from his neck and, shaking it into the air, shoo-shooed us away! He then turned and went back in. We stared up in disbelief at an empty balcony and then looked at one another, shrugged our shoulders, and left. We learned not to disturb an Italian at lunchtime. Dining is an event and should not be disturbed!

We had found our roots. It was such an exhilarating, emotional, and rewarding experience that it led to my increased yearning for everything Italian. It was like finding a treasure. From culture, art, music, wine, and history, I found a new path of exploration. When Elaine and I returned home, I visited my parents. I hugged and kissed my mother as usual. But this time for the first time I hugged and kissed my father. I told him we found Aunt Elena. It was the first time I ever saw my father's eyes tear up. We showed them photos and told them all our stories. I started a fresh search of my family's history. Elaine and I wrote an article for a new Italian magazine called *Attentzione*. For the first time in my life, I was proud to be Italian and not just in name only. That trip opened my eyes to being part of a beautiful culture. Growing up I think I took things for granted that my parents sacrificed for us. Getting older I realized how tough it must have been for my immigrant parents to overcome everything they endured. That may be the underlining reason why I continued to embrace my Italian heritage.

During this time I enrolled in a master's Program in Public Administration at Long Island University. While I was still working for NY State, one of my coworkers was Jim Brophy. We were having lunch one day and he told me he had a cousin, Jack Brophy, who was the chief U.S. Marshal in Manhattan. A few weeks later Jim called me over to his desk and told me he had been speaking to his cousin over the weekend and that Jack told him that the marshals were hiring and if he knew anyone to let him know. Jim asked if I would be interested. I had no idea what a marshal was but I told Jim I would be interested in finding out. Jim called his cousin Jack and put me on the phone with him. Jack explained that there was a fairly new Program that Congress passed a few years ago. The marshals were in charge of it and they would be hiring new employees. They needed more manpower to operate the Program. He asked me if I had college and the military. Jack told me I would have to take a nationwide test and be in a certain top percentage to be selected. Then I would have to go through interviews, background checks, medical and physical tests. I thanked him for the information. That new Program was the Witness Security Program.

Elaine and I talked about applying for the job as a deputy U.S. marshal. I did some looking into the job. I read a book called *The Alias Program* by reporter Phil Graham. It described some of the issues of this new Program. I applied for the job, took the exam, and got my first taste of the federal bureaucracy. That process took about a year. Finally, I was called for an interview in Manhattan in 1979. I went downtown Manhattan to the Marshals Office in the Southern District of New York for the interview. Also waiting to be interviewed was another candidate, XXX. On the interview panel was Augie Kaufman, John Steinhimer, and Jack Brophy. The interview went well. I was asked many questions about my application, my life experiences, my goals, my family, and my ability to work in different environments, with traveling and long hours. A few weeks later I received a letter congratulating me on my selection but I would still have to pass a physical exam, a medical and a background investigation. I was very thankful and thought that I was very lucky to be in the right place at the right time. Jim Brophy would ask me often about my progress with getting the job.

At this time, Elaine and I were expecting our first child. A letter came in the mail in April 1980 from the Marshals Service Headquarters in Washington, D.C. that I was scheduled for a medical exam in early May at 10 AM at 201 Varick Street, in Manhattan. Elaine and I were concerned because that was right around her due date. I called Marshals Service Personnel and asked if I rescheduled the exam how long would I have to wait for another date. I was advised that if I did not make the assigned date for the physical, it would knock me out of attending the next basic training class, which was scheduled for August. The person I spoke with said she could not confirm if I would be placed in another class. I discussed this with Elaine and we said we would wait and see when the baby would be born.

In early May on the night before the exam, Elaine said she would sleep in the other bedroom so I could get a good night's rest. I did but Elaine didn't. Unbeknownst to me she started having contractions during the night but didn't want to disturb me. Finally she came in the bedroom and woke me up at 5 AM, telling me, "We have to go to the hospital." We got to the hospital on time. We had taken Lamaze classes in preparation for the birth but the baby wasn't ready. Now it was 8 AM and we talked about what I should do. The doctors and the nurses said it could be a few hours but not sure. We decided that I would go to the physical and then return. I waited for a while with Elaine but she told me to go. When I pulled into the parking garage near 201 Varick Street, I took my parking stub, went in, and called the hospital. The nurse told me I was the father of a beautiful girl. I talked to Elaine, who was fine. I then took my physical and returned to the hospital. When I asked the time of birth, it was the same time as on my parking stub!

A few weeks later I received a notice from the Marshals to report for duty on August 10, 1980. All in all it was about two years before I was hired. I gave NY State a resignation letter and I was on my way to be a federal marshal. Little did I know at that time that I would have the career of a lifetime and be a little part of history.

XXX and I both were hired together and reported the same day. We had a good laugh. The day of the interview, XXX was wearing a regular shirt with no tie or jacket. The panel asked him why he showed up without proper attire. He told them he just got out of the military and did not own a tie or a jacket. They accepted his response but informed him of the dress code. We worked for a couple of weeks together to get processed into the job and then got orders to report to the Federal Law Enforcement Training Center (FLETC) in Georgia for training.

XXX had asked me if he could get a ride to the airport for the trip south. I picked him up on the side of the road, off Rt. 95 in the Bronx. He was carrying an Army duffel bag with him. For the next three months we would be in FLETC going through Criminal Investigator School and Basic Training. It was like being back in the military. It was mostly physical tests, firing various weapons, high-speed driving, legal classes, classroom instruction, and role playing.

After completion of the schools, I returned home in late October. I will never forget that moment. Catherine was three months old when I left and twice as old at six months when I returned. When I walked into the living room, Elaine was holding Catherine, telling her, "Daddy's home!" Catherine took one look at me and started crying! I had some time to make up. After I was selected for the job and started working, I told my parents of my new job. They had no idea about the type of work I would be doing. I told them I would be carrying a gun but I didn't tell them that I would be dealing with violent criminals or searching for fugitives. My mother was shocked. My father didn't say a word. He just smiled and nodded his head in approval. No one in our family had ever been in law enforcement before.

3

The United States Marshals Service

"There is fear in every man; the important thing is that it is accompanied by courage."

Paolo Borsellino

The Marshals Service has a long and distinguished history. It is the oldest federal law enforcement agency in the country. The Judiciary Act of 1789, created by the first Congress, established the U.S. Marshals Office. President George Washington appointed the first 13 U.S. marshals, one for each of the original colonies. They were given extensive authority to carry out all lawful orders issued by the courts, Congress, and the President. Today, the U.S. marshal position is still a presidential appointment. The year 2014 marked the 225th anniversary of the U.S. Marshals Service. To celebrate, the U.S. Mint had a commemorative silver dollar created for the occasion in 2015. Stacy Hylton, the director of the Marshals Service at that time, visited the mint at West Point. That is the same mint where my father worked. And by the way, that was the same year that I attended my 50th high school class reunion!

When I first arrived at the Marshals Office in 1979 for my initial job interview, I was amazed at the number of government buildings comprising the area called Foley Square. I was not that familiar with the area, even though it is only a few blocks from Chinatown and Little Italy, where I had visited previously. At the time I didn't know I would be spending the next twenty-three years of my life working, enjoying, and learning the history of the area.

My new office was on the second floor of the building that housed the United States Attorney's Office for the Southern District of New York. One of my duties was escorting inmates from MCC to court appearances for trials, hearings, arrangements, and sentencings. The district has the reputation of being one of the busiest in the country.

After working in the area, I would often walk through Foley Square and admire how the buildings were squeezed into the square. The courthouse at 40 Foley was built in 1936 and was designed by Cass Gilbert, who also designed the U.S. Custom House, the Woolworth Building a few blocks away, and the U.S. Supreme Court Building in D.C. Foley Square, which is just a few blocks north of City Hall, was named after Thomas F. Foley, a saloon-keeper and prominent district leader of the political group Tammany Hall. The courthouse stands between the New York State Supreme Court Building and the forty-story Municipal Building. Admiring 40 Foley's massive Minnesota granite staircase with Corinthian columns, your eye also continues along to the columns of the State Court Building. I would recommend this area for a tourist to explore: If you stop and admire these massive buildings, you have to remember one thing. This area was the former Five Points District made famous in the movie *Gangs of New York*. The district was infamous as one of the poorest and most dangerous slums in the world, first accommodating many breweries and tanneries, and then a massive prison called the Tombs, and then livestock slaughter-houses. Charles Dickens described the area in lurid prose after an 1842 visit: "This is the place: these narrow ways, diverging to the right and left, and reeking everywhere with dirt and filth."[2]

The United States Court of the District of New York, predecessor to the Southern District of New York, was created in the same year as the Marshals Service. The Southern District covers Manhattan, the Bronx, Westchester, Putnam, Dutchess, Rockland, Orange, and Sullivan Counties. In 1983, a U.S. courthouse was opened in a leased former IBM building in White Plains, NY, in Westchester County. The Honorable Lee P. Gagliardi was the only presiding District Court judge at the time in the new courthouse. He was from the area and was instrumental in getting the courthouse located there to accommodate jurors from the upstate counties so they would not have to travel to downtown Manhattan.

One day Chief XXX called me into his office. He asked if I wanted to report to the office in White Plains that would be opening soon. He told me I would have a G-car that I could take home, and it would be a better commute. I said yes. After the new courthouse opened, the late Joe Nicotina and I were the only marshals who reported to the new sub-office at White Plains. At the time it was very slow and there wasn't much work there. I ended up working there for only a few months and then was moved back downtown. I didn't mind because I wanted more experience and it was busier.

At this time there was a dramatic increase in cases and trials. There was also an increase in the hiring of agents, prosecutors, and judges. As a result, space was limited both at 40 Foley and White Plains. To address this situation, new courthouses were built. In the mid-1990s, the Charles Brieant Federal Courthouse was built in White Plains near the other local state and city courthouses. At the same time, the Daniel Patrick Moynihan Courthouse was constructed at 500 Pearl Street. It was squeezed into a former parking lot behind the State courthouse. I remember in the mornings when I parked my G-car in a garage on Worth Street and walked through that lot, there were many Asian senior citizens exercising by performing Tai Chi.

In 2006, the old courthouse was closed for renovation and re-opened in 2013. In June of 2015, Southern District Marshals Office held its reunion at the old federal courthouse at 40 Foley Square. It had been renamed the Thurgood Marshall Courthouse in honor of the late Supreme Court justice. I was happy to attend the reunion to socialize with friends and coworkers I hadn't seen in years. We were also given a tour of the renovated courthouse by personnel from the Second Circuit Court of Appeals, whose home is also in the building. A photo of all was taken in one of the renovated courtrooms.

Some of the country's most prominent cases on a variety of is-sues have taken place in 40 Foley. Well-known espionage and ter-rorism trials, criminal prosecutions, important First Amendment cases, and celebrity cases have been heard there. Personally, I was involved in mob cases, including the trials of the Pizza Connection case, the Commission case, the Castellano case, and many, many more.

Tucked away behind the courthouse facing the plaza is St. Andrew's Roman Catholic Church. It is in the alleyway between the courthouse and 1 St. Andrew's Plaza. I have spent much time in this church, attending Mass, going to confession, and even attend-ing Christmas parties in the basement sponsored by the Marshals, the U.S. Attorney's Office, and other agencies. This church serves the needs of workers in the area and local neighborhoods. My friend and former deputy coworker Dennis DeFabbio and I would support the church lunch Program—good spaghetti and meatballs made and served by local Italian women. The church would also have an an-nual Memorial Mass for law enforcement personnel.

On January 11, 1794, U.S. Marshal Robert Forsyth of Georgia was the first civilian official of the United States government killed in the line of duty. Since then, over 200 marshals have been killed in the past 225 years. While I was writing this book, USMS personnel called me to let me know a DUSM was killed in the line of duty. On March 10, 2015, Deputy U.S. Marshal Josie Wells was killed while part of an arrest team that went to a motel in Baton Rouge, Louisiana, to arrest a fugitive wanted for a double homicide. When the marshals burst through the door, the fugitive shot Wells in the neck. The fugitive was shot and killed. Wells was a native of Mississippi. He was a black 27-year-old college graduate from a law enforcement family. His wife was expecting their first child. This incident didn't get much national news coverage. It occurred a few weeks before the riots in Baltimore saturated the news. It appears that the bad elements of society get more news coverage than the good guys.

On November 18, 2016, Deputy United States Marshal Patrick Carothers was killed in the line of duty while executing an arrest warrant in Georgia. He was a twenty-six-year veteran of the USMS. He left a wife and five children. My prayers go out to the families of these slain marshals.

In 1980, when I returned from basic training, I was like all other new personnel, assigned to general duties. However, when assigned to Witness Security details, it was for two weeks, seven days a week, twelve hours a day. XXX was the chief inspector of Wit/Sec at the time.

My first assignment in Wit/Sec was for the protection of a witness testifying in the trial of Funzi Tieri. At that time, Tieri was the boss of the Genovese organized crime family. I remember the elder Tieri, wearing sunglasses, being wheeled into the courtroom by a nurse dressed in white. Tieri was the first organized crime (OC) boss to be convicted under the new Racketeer Influenced and Corrupt Organizations Act (RICO) law. That was the new and most effective tool given to the U.S. Attorney's. He was sentenced to ten years. Tieri passed away in jail about a year later.

My first high-profile motorcade was on a Wit/Sec detail. I was assigned to the protective detail of Edwin Wilson, the rogue ex-CIA agent who was arrested for arms dealing in the Middle East. After his arrest I don't think the government knew what his status was going to be. So, instead of him being held in a federal lockup awaiting trial, he was coming to New York to be held in a safe house. At daylight we went down to the Wall Street heliport where Wilson would be arriving from D.C. Arrangements were made to clear the air space over lower Manhattan. As we waited, we received communications from the detail with Wilson that they would be arriving in five minutes. From the heliport we could see two Army Cobra gunship helicopters flying low above the water, coming around Governors Island. One gunship circled the area while the other landed. We took custody of Wilson and drove to the safe house. I was driving the follow car. Inspector XXX was with me. XXX was born in Val di Non, Trentino, which is the next mountain valley west of Val di Fiemma, where my father was born.

Working the Wit/Sec detail included a lot of traveling. One day I was scheduled to take a prisoner witness for a trip out of Newark Airport. Another marshal and I were getting the witness ready to depart for the airport. The witness asked me what district I was from and where we were leaving from. I told him I was from SDNY and we were going to Newark, New Jersey. The witness advised me that he refused to travel in New Jersey with any marshal. I asked him why. He informed me that New Jersey had a problem with corrupt marshals. I told him to sit tight and I went and advised Chief XXX. He told me he would go and talk to the witness. After a few minutes

XXX came out and instructed us to change our flight plans and fly out of a New York airport. A few days later I asked him what that was all about, and he said it was a misunderstanding. He said a rumor had been going around, but there was nothing to it. I never heard anything about it after that incident.

Over the next few years, I had some enjoyable experiences working with some good investigators, especially in the Warrant Squad. To some investigators there is no greater challenge than hunting down another man. The ones who are successful are the ones who can control their emotions. They are the ones who overcome their fear and have the courage to do the job. It can be a rough-and-tumble world. It is not unusual to end up rolling around on the ground trying to arrest someone who is not willing to go peacefully. Knocking down doors, raiding apartments at daybreak, chasing fugitives down alleyways, shootouts—those are the scenes you always see in the movies and on the TV cop shows. In reality, the number of times a federal agent discharges his weapon is minimal. I learned about expecting the unexpected. No matter how many plans are made, I always was intrigued by the reaction of unexpected events.

The procedure at the time in the Warrant Squad was that there were some permanent personnel and then others would rotate every three months. One time I was in the squad working my three-month rotation with Bill Fitzgerald. Bill had joined the Marshals just a few years before me, and we lived near one another. One of the unique aspects of hunting fugitives is that law enforcement usually has one advantage. You know what the fugitive looks like, including their physical characteristics (tattoos, scars, etc.). The fugitive does not know the hunter's description.

For example, we had a warrant for a very heavyset black woman who ran a fraudulent check-cashing scam. She employed a dozen or so women who were flooding Orange County with fake checks. They were making thousands of dollars a week. One evening Bill and I were leaving work and walking up Baxter Street in lower Manhattan on our way to get our assigned vehicle, aka "The G Ride," when we saw the woman we were looking for. She had walked out of a law office and just about bumped into us on the sidewalk. She had no idea who we were. We stopped and looked at one another and then turned around in disbelief. We walked down the street behind her to see where she was going or if anyone was with her. We arrested her when she was going to her car. The woman was at the wrong place at the wrong time. By the time we remanded her to the Metropolitan Correctional Center (MCC), it turned out to be a very late night.

There were very rare times when you had a warrant for someone with just a description and no photograph. That changes the odds in catching someone. One day I was working in the Warrant Squad office, and the supervisor, Frank Devlin, came over to my desk. He told me he just received a warrant for a guy and assigned it to me. The guy was involved in a civil case with Judge Sofaer, SDNY, and was ordered to pay a $25,000 fine on the case. The guy failed to pay the fine. He was the son of a NYC businessman who was wealthy, and he was the rich playboy son. The first thing I had to do was find a photo of the guy because he had never been arrested, never been processed, and there was no photo of him. A few days later I asked Augie Kaufmann and Willie Brown, two other marshals in the Warrant Squad, to come with me to Queens where the guy had an office in a real estate company. Augie and Willie interviewed workers in the real estate office while I went into the guy's office. Behind his desk on the wall were numerous photos of celebrities. I "borrowed" an autographed picture off the wall of the guy with Senator Ted Kennedy. I stuck it under my shirt in my back and we left. Today, you could take out your iPhone and snap a shot! Weeks later I found out that the fugitive was on an African safari. I placed his personal information on the Immigration and Customs lookout list. A few days later I got a notification that he was arrested at the border in upstate New York. The fugitive flew into Canada from his safari and rented a car to drive across the border to come back to New York, expecting to sneak back into the States. The judge ordered that the guy be put on a prison bus and take the longest route from the border to NYC.

A few times I also worked with Bill Huffnagel and John Cuff, known throughout the law enforcement community as "Huff and Cuff." They created a dynasty in establishing a very professional and well-known Electronic Surveillance Unit in Headquarters in D.C. They had started accumulating equipment in a closet in the Warrant Squad in Southern District. Years later Huff would go to Headquarters to create, manage, and expand the unit. Cuff stayed in New York and New Jersey.

Cuff and I were teamed up in the Warrant Squad for our rotation. We were working on a case of a fugitive who was known to hang out around 145th Street and Lenox Avenue in Harlem. "Blood" had a long, violent arrest record. We went uptown after interviewing some people and found out that Blood would frequent a bar on 145th Street late at night. Across the street from the bar was a boxing club on the second floor that overlooked the bar across the street. We checked out the club and the management. It would be a perfect place to set up surveillance. The next day we approached the manager. He told us he closed the club at 10 PM and we could use the place all night. He never asked us any questions. He just gave us a key. We told him it might be in a week or so. Frank Devlin authorized us to set up in the club.

One Friday summer night John and I set up on the second floor. Frank and another team were around the corner from the bar. We had binoculars to watch individuals entering and leaving the bar. It was after midnight when an old drunk man staggered to the middle of 145th Street as cars were speeding past, beeping at him. He stood there yelling, "FBI, FBI, the FBI is going to get all you no-good bastards!" The people on the streets yelled at him to shut up and get off the street. He staggered around. Just around then, John spotted a guy who looked like Blood come out of the bar and walk toward the corner. We called Frank with a description of what he was wearing. The two cars pulled up to a screeching halt, grabbed him, and threw him in the backseat and took off. It turned out to be the wrong guy! It wasn't Blood. The guy was let go a few blocks away. The old drunk came back out into the street yelling, "I told you dumb bastards the FBI was going to get y'all!" John and I went out the back alleyway to our car and we could still hear the old man yelling "FBI" ringing in our ears! Sometimes even the best plans do not pan out.

Another time, Huff had been looking for a prostitute who was wanted for failure to appear in a large-scale drug case. He asked me to go with him over to Long Island City, where this girl was known to frequent. It was a hot summer day and we were interviewing different people in various locations. Huff was driving and we stopped at a bodega to get something to drink. I went in and Huff stayed in the "G ride." As I walked in, I spotted the girl we were looking for at the register buying cigarettes. She started walking toward the door and I stopped her. I ID'd myself to her. She was upset. I showed her the car outside. Huff was parked past the doorway and couldn't see us. We walked to the car and I opened the back door for the girl. Huff turned around and did a double take. "What happened?" That's all he could say on the way back to the office as the girl wouldn't stop asking Huff to please talk to the judge. Huff just kept looking at me. She also was in the wrong place at the wrong time.

Huff developed information that a fugitive would be visiting a girlfriend in her expensive high-rise apartment on East 79th Street in the afternoon. We went uptown on a nice spring day. We showed a picture of the fugitive to the doorman, who verified that the guy came by around 3 PM some days to visit a girl in the building. We advised the doorman that we would be parked across the street and when the guy showed up to step out and take his hat off. The doorman said he would keep the door wide open since it was a nice day. We set up across the street and waited. After about a half hour we watched a shirtless old man with his pants down around his knees urinating on the front of the apartment building we were watching. He started staggering toward the building entrance. We were saying, "Don't go in. Don't go in." The man slowly took a few steps and then stopped. He tried to go in one direction and reversed and started toward the building again. "Don't go in! Don't go in!" we were shouting! He took a few more steps and was now under the awning. The doorman was inside and did not see the man. Huff was hoping that the man did not go in the building, but sure enough, the man picked up speed and ran straight into the lobby of the apartment building and collapsed on the lobby's marble floor with his pants down around his ankles. The doorman came running outside, taking his hat off and on and waving for us to come over. We knew this man wasn't the fugitive! We knew the doorman was doing the right thing by us, so we had to help him. We crossed the street and went into the lobby with the doorman, who was cursing and asking us to drag the man outside. Huff checked the man out on the floor, looked up at me, and said, "He is DOA!"

We told the doorman to call an ambulance. There was no one around in the lobby. The doorman kept asking us just to drag him out to the street! We told him he was dead and that we could not move him. We were standing next to the dead man on the lobby floor when the elevator door opened. A very proper, coiffured elderly woman walking a poodle came out of the elevator and saw the half-naked man lying on the lobby floor. She screamed and said, "Who is that?"

I told her, "It is your new super." A little gallows humor can go a long way. She gasped and turned around and got back on the elevator. NYPD and an ambulance showed up, but our fugitive did not. The fugitive wasn't apprehended that day, but his day would come.

One morning I was walking into the office as Frank Devlin was hastily leaving. He told me, "Come on, SADDLE UP! We are going to the Bronx." We ran outside and got in his vehicle and departed using the emergency equipment. On the way he told me Tommy Higgins just called. Higgins was also in the squad and to put it mildly he was a very excitable person. Tommy called to say one of his informants called him to say a guy Tommy was looking for was sitting on a stoop in a Bronx neighborhood. The fugitive was wearing a red shirt. Tommy was way out on Long Island and said it would take him awhile to get to the Bronx. While Frank and I were on our way, Tommy kept calling us to see if we got there yet!

A few blocks away from the area, we turned off the lights and siren. We turned onto the block where the fugitive was, and it was a one-way street. We saw the guy in the red shirt stand up from the stoop and look at us. He started running. However, he ran the wrong way. He ran in the direction we were traveling. We were driving down the street alongside him as he was running on the sidewalk. I had the passenger door open as we were moving along. The guy turned and ran into a residential building. Frank stopped the car and I chased the guy into the building. He went downstairs and as I was running down I heard a door slam. I followed him through a basement and out another door into a backyard. When I exited the building, there was a chain-link fence a few yards away from the building. The guy was just at the top of the fence with one leg over when I jumped and grabbed his other leg. When I pulled him down, his pant leg that was on the top of the fence got caught in the fence, and he was hanging upside down. The guy was screaming.

As I tussled with him, I told him to put his hands together. I cuffed him. I told him to relax; I was going to rip his pant leg off to release him from the fence. That was the first and last time I ever cuffed a guy who was upside down! Just then I could hear Frank calling me. I told him where I was. When he showed up he couldn't believe the guy was on the ground cuffed with half his pant leg ripped off. When we got back in the car, Tommy was still calling, saying he was twenty minutes away. Frank told him to slow down and disregard. We had the guy in custody and we were headed back downtown. Sometime later Frank was selected as the USMS representative to INTERPOL and was reassigned overseas to France.

Don Ward also worked in the Warrant Squad. Don called me one day to say Bill Fitzgerald and he were looking for a Colombian drug dealer whose wife and children were living in the town where I was living. I told them I didn't recognize the name, but I would ask Elaine because she was teaching in the local school and knew more of the families than I did. It was summertime and I asked Elaine, but she didn't know them. She said she would check when school was back in session.

School started soon after, and Elaine told me that one of the sons of the fugitive was in her class. Elaine gave the typical back-to-school writing assignment, "My Summer Vacation." The boy wrote that he had gone to his brother's funeral. His brother was visiting their father in a city down south and was killed in an accident. I notified Don, who contacted the marshals in the father's area. The local marshals found the funeral home the father used, which listed his home address. A team of marshals went to the house where the father was living. However, the father was able to escape out a back window. Shortly thereafter he was arrested. After this incident I would kid Elaine and tell her I never thought I would marry a federal informant!

It was right around this time when I understood it was common practice to socialize after work. One day I was leaving work when I saw Chief XXX. He told me some people were getting together at a local restaurant and invited me to join them. When I arrived the chief introduced me to John Martin, who at the time was the U.S. Attorney for the Southern District. John was very polite and asked how my family was and we talked for a few minutes. The next day the chief called me and asked how I knew John Martin. I told him we grew up in the same area and our families went to school together. XXX asked me if I ever wanted to put in for a job in Headquarters or any district to let him know and he would make a call for me. I never had any intentions of leaving New York and uprooting my family for the job. Some people make that move to Headquarters for a promotion. Some survive and stay there. Others have to find another home and then make another move. Either way did not interest me. I thanked XXX for thinking of me anyway.

A few years later in 1990, John Martin was sworn in as a U.S. District Court judge in SDNY. I attended his swearing in and talked to his brother Frank for the first time since grammar school. Frank was an attorney in Washington. Later on you will read about another conversation I had with Frank in which, I am sorry to say, there was an unpleasant ending.

In 1983, I was working on a Saturday. Bob Wilmoth was my supervisor and told me I had a phone call. It was my brother Sal. He told me that Dad had just passed away in the hospital. I informed Wilmoth, who told me to leave and asked if I wanted to take one of the G-cars home. I told him no, I would need to be off for the following week, and he approved my leave. I got on the subway and took a Metro North train home.

I sat on that train looking out at the Hudson River as many thoughts of my father's life passed by. He had gone into the hospital a few days before because of an aneurism. My father was the type who did not like hospitals or doctors. He told me once he was put in a hospital and jumped out of the second-floor window. If my father wasn't feeling well, my mother would call Dr. Margolis, who at that time was our family doctor and who made house calls. I could see Dr. Margolis walking into the house shaking his head in a depressed state because he knew he would have to put up with my father, who would object to everything Dr. Margolis recommended. The doctor knew my father would not take any medicine, so when he showed up, he and my father would sit at the kitchen table and have a shot of Canadian Club whiskey. When it was time to leave, my father would tell the doctor, "If you leave any medicine with my wife, I will throw it in the garbage."

He was a hard worker with a ready laugh and was very well liked. He worked as the all-around maintenance man for many years at the U.S. Mint at West Point. He told me the following story. The mint, which is a secure facility with a chain-link fence and security, is located next to the West Point ski slope. One day my father was out in the yard of the mint and he noticed a skier coming down the slope. The skier fell, went off the ski trail, and landed near the fence of the mint. My father yelled at him, "Hey, what's wrong? You can't stay up on your feet?!"

Well, the skier went over to the fence and yelled at my father, "What's your name?"

My father said, "Who the hell are you?"

The skier replied, "I'm General Westmoreland!"

My father replied, "Good to meet you because I have something to talk to you about."

Westmoreland told my father that he had never been to the mint and wanted to get a tour. My father told him, "When you are finished skiing and you can stay on your feet, come over and I will give you a tour." Westmorland laughed and came back. My father and his boss gave him the tour.

Finally, my father was able to talk to him about a pressing issue in our household that was troubling my mother. "I have a son who is a plebe at West Point, and he is losing weight because of the way he has to square his meals; they give him only a few minutes to eat and then he has to run to class. His mother is worried about his health. In the meantime, the other cadets on sports teams can eat more and there are fewer restrictions on them. Can you see what you can do for him?"

Shortly thereafter my brother was made manager of the golf team. He got to sit and eat at the athletes' table. He put on a few pounds and made his Sicilian mother happy, knowing that he was eating well.

My father didn't own a car. He would car pool with some other workers and would get dropped off on the corner of the street where we lived. I remember as a kid seeing my father happily walking home whistling, carrying his brown lunch bag with the *NY Daily News* sticking out. Growing up, I loved to read the newspaper and would run to meet him and jump up and grab the paper, which he would let me carry home for him. Some days his bosses from the New York Essay Office would visit our house when they had to make official visits to the mint. They would drive my father home, drink, and talk about their work. My mother would make food for them and they enjoyed it. I remember one of the big bosses was Mr. Edwards. When my father retired in 1969, he was presented with a gold watch that was left to me. After my father retired, his old bosses would still stop by the house and visit. For his services, he was presented with the United States Treasury Department's Albert Gallatin Award. Albert Gallatin was Secretary of the Treasury from 1801 to 1814.

As a part-time electrician, my father would help anyone who needed something fixed. However, people would telephone the house at all hours for his services. If he was tired or didn't want to talk, he would tell us kids not to answer the phone. Or if one of us kids picked up the phone, he would say, "Tell them I'm not home!" My loving mother would say, "That's not nice. You are teaching the kids to lie." That would set him off with another round of explosive, creative language. However, he was always willing to help anyone. He did not care about getting paid for his services so long as he helped that person. Sometimes after working a job, he would come home with a bushel of apples as his pay. In the meantime, my mother was trying to put food on the table to feed six kids! My sister Jacque has a large painting, which was payment for one of my father's jobs. And, of course, all of us kids had friends who we would have over to eat at our house.

When he finished a big electric job, he would sign the panel box "Wire Dapra - 100,000 satisfied customers coast to coast." He lived a happy life for eighty years. He was very knowledgeable about electronics and enjoyed reading about electric inventions. In the 1950s, he wired a few houses and converted the electricity to low voltage for touch plate switches. At the time it was a very advanced, modern system. There was a panel in the bedroom that displayed tiny red lights representing a light in each room of the house. When you went to bed, you could see if a light was still on in another room. Consequently, you wouldn't have to get up to go turn off any lights in the rest of the house. You just pushed the little indicator, and the light in the other room would go out. I live in one of those houses today. I just wish that he had lived to experience the Internet and our present wireless world.

At this time in my career with the marshals, I missed the birth of our first child and missed being at the bedside for the passing of my father. And so far I had only been working with them for three years.

In 1984, I was assigned to a Fugitive Investigative Strike Team (FIST). Around this time period, the Marshals Service would select different areas of the country to assist local law enforcement in reducing the number of outstanding warrants. For this FIST operation, our command center was at Fort Totten near the Whitestone Bridge. Other USMS personnel from around the country came into New York to assist NYPD in clearing up their outstanding felony warrants. It lasted a few weeks. There were a few other FIST operations over the years around the country. During my time on the team, I was partners with NYPD Detective John McDonald, who lived in Bay Ridge, Brooklyn. Every morning at seven I would pick him up on Third Avenue. John and I got along well and made our share of arrests. These operations were number games. There were no long-term investigations. That wasn't the purpose. The mission was clearing out old and new outstanding warrants for city and federal cases. At one time or another most of the Eastern District and Southern District Warrant Squad members were on FIST operations around the country, where there were thousands of arrests being made not only for outstanding warrants but also for murder, weapons, and drugs.

While I was working for Southern District, one morning my supervisor, Bob Wilmoth, called me in his office to give me an assignment. He told me he was short of personnel and didn't have anyone else to go with me. He instructed me to take Michele Sindona, who was incarcerated at the federal Metropolitan Correctional Center (MCC), to pre-trial services. Bob advised me that when other personnel became available, he would send them to assist me. I went to the cell block area where Sindona was in a holding pen. I handcuffed him and escorted him to the pre-trial services office and when I got there the clerk put us in a private room. Another clerk came in and gave Sindona his pre-sentence report to read. The clerk also gave me a copy and said, "You're his attorney, right?"

I said, "No."

Sindona looked at her and shook his head no. He was known as the "Vatican Banker" and had been indicted for fraud in the biggest bank failure in U.S. history. Sindona had bankrupted the Long Island Franklin National Bank after buying controlling interest from Lawrence Tisch, Loews Corporation. Sindona showed up with a gunshot wound in midtown, claiming to have been kidnapped. He was also wanted in Italy for murder and bank fraud. Sindona was considered a major money launderer for the Sicilian Mafia. He was sentenced to twenty-five years to life in Southern District. In the fall of 1984, he was extradited to Italy to stand trial there and was convicted. A few days after his conviction in Italy, Sindona was drinking a cup of coffee in his prison cell. He was found dead from cyanide poisoning.

In 1984, I received a call from Larry Parker. Larry was from Eastern District of New York in Brooklyn but had taken a job as an instructor at the training site in Glynco, Georgia. He asked me to come down and be a counselor for a basic class he would be teaching. I told him I would think about it and he said he would have to get the okay from the chief. I talked to Elaine. It would be for a couple of weeks. I called Larry and we worked it out. I went there and enjoyed interacting with the class. I had to work out with the new recruits and run with them. When I was in my basic class, I was considered older because of my four years of military service. Now I had an additional four years since I went through my own basic training with the USMS. It was easier to keep in shape there than when working different hours and traveling in New York. Besides the physical aspects, there was a lot of new training in shoot and don't shoot scenarios. There were empty houses that were used for tactics for searching for armed fugitives.

The training center at Glynco hired real actors from the area as role players for training purposes. On one occasion deputies were to raid a house looking for counterfeit money. It was a household of four people and there were a handful of deputies who had a raid plan and assigned duties on the raid. One of the new recruits was a female from Newark, New Jersey. Her role was to keep the family in the living room in their seats while the search team looked through the house. One of the role players kept telling the female recruit that she wanted to get up to go to the bathroom. The recruit told her she could not. The woman persisted and told the recruit she was going to get up and go to the bathroom. The recruit told her, "If you get up, I will shoot you!" That's all the role player had to hear. She stood up and the recruit took out her gun with blanks in it and shot the role player! The exercise was stopped. The female recruit was interviewed by the instructors and the Academy higher-ups. The next day the recruit was on a plane back to Newark. She didn't get the job.

Another member of the basic training class was XXX, who was from New Jersey and who was being assigned to SDNY. Years later XXX and I would end up working together. At graduation the class presented me with a plaque that read, "Thanks for helping us to give our best." Working with Larry Parker and the other new recruits was a very positive experience for me. In later years I would end up meeting and sometimes working with those new deputies in their respective districts throughout the United States.

By 1985, Jack Brophy was no longer chief in New York. He had gone to law school at night and received his law degree. Jack left government and moved to San Francisco to practice law. There was a major personnel shuffle. XXX, who was the chief of Witness Security, replaced Jack Brophy as chief of Southern District. XXX took over as chief of Witness Security. His assistant was XXX. XXX and XXX had been in Wit/Sec for years. One day while I was on a Witness Security detail, XXX called me in his office and closed the door. He told me there were going to be two openings in the office. These Wit/Sec positions in New York were highly sought after and competitive. The office had a good reputation. XXX was recommending XXX and me for the positions as inspectors. XXX was also a deputy in Southern District at the time. He told me he cleared it with Howard Safir, associate director of operations in Headquarters. I had to tell him yes or no by the next day. He said there would be no job opening announcement for the positions or interviews. There would only be a teletype coming out making the announcement. I shook XXX's hand and thanked him for considering me. When I walked out of the office, XXX came up to me and said, "You better say yes!"

This is a copy of my grandmother's passport photo when she left Sicily for America in 1921 with her children. My mother is on the left, standing in front of her mother, Marietta Buonsigore Graziano. Standing next to my mother is her brother, Colegero (Lee). In front in the middle is my mother's sister Rose (my godmother). Also with them on the journey was my mother's oldest sister, Josephine, who was sixteen years old and had to have a separate photo, included with this passport.

My father, Lorenzo, with his parents, Rosa Vanzo and Gilberto.

My parents wedding day in front of Sacred Heart Church. June 19th, 1938.

My brothers from left to right, Larry, Sal, and Lee, with me looking up to my big brothers in my white Communion suit. Behind my brothers in the background are my sisters, Jacque and Margie, with our cousin Barbara. I made my first Holy Communion on May 21, 1955.

Korea, 1970. With a Korean orphan I "adopted" for the day in Kuang Ju. I brought her on base to the chow hall for Thanksgiving Day dinner. I'm carrying a goody bag for her.

The Plaza Hotel. This is part of the famous Oak Bar that is now closed at the Plaza, where I enjoyed stopping when I worked in the hotel. The Fairmont Hotel chain managed the property at this time. All Rights Reserved.

This is a photo I took from the top of 20 Exchange Place downtown during the celebration of "Liberty Weekend" in 1986 on the detail with Supreme Court Chief Justice Warren Berger. This photo shows the Statue of Liberty "ablaze" from the amount of smoke and fireworks at the base of the statue. The arm of the statue is just visible reaching out to the masses. You can also see the number of boats in the harbor and the "frozen zone" around the statue where boats were not allowed to get too close.

In front of Gioielleria DiPaola, Palermo, Sicily, 1997, with Gabriella Giuntini, Polizia de Stato. Gabriella knew the owner. I bought Elaine jewelry here. Unbeknown to me Gabriella bought items for my daughters, Catherine and Theresa, and had the jewelry delivered to my hotel room.

Palermo, Sicily, 1997. Left to right, Pat Fitzgerald, AUSA, SDNY; Antonio Maganelli, Questora of Palermo; me; Santi Giuffre, Chief Polizia di Stato. Photo taken in Maganelli's private residence. Maganelli is now deceased.

In 1982, Calogero Zucchetto, an agent with the Polizia di Stato, was shot and killed in Palermo. I came across this memorial for him one evening in Palermo. You can see the fresh floral display. The plaque reads that he was assassinated at the hands of the Mafia. There are other memorials in Palermo for the many policemen and judges killed in their war against the Mafia.

This photo was taken of me at the 20th Anniversary of the Witness Security Program in the lobby of the old United States Courthouse, 40 Foley Square. The photo was taken by Jim Nauwens, Investigator U.S. Attorney's Office, SDNY, 1991.

This is the flag of the region of Trentino. When I visited the Office of the Provincia Autonoma in Trento, I was presented with this flag and books on the history of the region. The flag measures three feet by five feet.

"The symbol of Trento is the fiery eagle of St. Wenceslas, King of Bohemia, reproduced from the original warrant of 10 August 1939 with which the Chancellor of Luxembourg granted its use to the Prince-Bishop of Trento, Nicolo di Bruna."

—From the last page of the atlas *Beautiful Trentino*, Published by Panorama Publishers, Trento, Italy. All Rights Reserved.

4

WIT/SEC World

"You live by the gun and knife, and die by the gun and knife."

—Joe Valachi

The Witness Security Program was officially created when Congress passed the Organized Crime Control Act of 1970 and enacted it in 1971. The Program guidelines are spelled out in United States Code 18, Chapter 224, and Sections: 3521-3528.

The Program consists of two phases. In Phase 1 are prisoner witnesses (PWs). These are cooperating witnesses for the government, but they are incarcerated. This Program is run by the Bureau of Prisons (BOP). There are certain BOP prison facilities throughout the U.S. where PWs are held in special units separate from the general population of the prison. At the time of a PW's release, if he wants to apply for Phase II of the USMS Wit/Sec Program, he would have to make a formal application and be sponsored by an assistant U.S. attorney and go through the lengthy application process. It consists of a preliminary interview, threat assessments, psychological testing, and completing the U.S. Attorney application form. All that information is submitted to the United States Attorney General's Office.

The Office of Enforcement Operations (OEO), acting for the Attorney General of the United States, is authorized to provide for the security and safety of any government witness and family members who voluntarily enter the Program. The witnesses would have to agree to testify truthfully whenever called upon. They would have to agree to be relocated to a place of safety, provided a new identity in order to become self-sufficient, and assimilate back into society.

Prior to the Program being created, no witnesses were coming forward in organized crime cases for fear of being murdered. Organized crime's most effective tool against being prosecuted was killing anyone brave enough to testify in a trial.

The Program's top selling point has been that in its history, no one in the Program who has followed all the rules and regulations has ever been killed.

When the Department of Justice focuses on a particular individual as a target in a criminal investigation, they shine a spotlight on that person, looking to get all the information of criminal activity for a conviction in court. However, that spotlight does not always illuminate secret corners of that individual's life. That's where co-operating witnesses entrenched in organizations and participating in criminal activities become important sources for revealing secrets. Sometimes these witnesses turn out to be family members of the target. In some rare cases they are also undercover agents.

The early days of the Program in the 1970s coincided with growing awareness of the Italian-American gangster in the movies, books, and television. The bestselling book by Mario Puzo, *The Godfather*, was out around the same time the Program was created. One might say *The Godfather* and the Program made their debut together. The American public became fascinated with the life of crime as depicted by Hollywood.

In 1971, Joe Colombo, of the Colombo crime family, picketed the FBI offices in New York and claimed discrimination against Italian-Americans and a violation of civil rights. Colombo formed the Italian-American Civil Rights League. Colombo was attempting to get support from honest, hardworking Italian-Americans. During the infamous Columbus Day rally at Columbus Circle, Colombo was shot. His shooter was shot and killed. Colombo survived, although paralyzed, and died years later at his home in Washingtonville, New York.

Personally, the 1970s atmosphere set the stage for my own interest in all things Italian and for a career in law enforcement. I had discovered my roots in that wonderful trip to Italy with Elaine. I had become interested in the Marshals and the new Program by talking to Chief Brophy. I started doing my homework about the Program and the many problems the Marshals faced in operating something that had never existed before and in carrying out their assigned mission. I was just learning about the impact organized crime had on society and the Italian-American community. It was becoming more apparent that Hollywood was making movies depicting gangsters in a more favorable light. The bad guys were becoming the good guys. The roles were getting reversed.

In April 1985, I was promoted to Witness Security inspector. The position of inspector was created to establish a specialty in the division of the U.S. Marshals tasked with the protection of government witnesses who receive new identities and are relocated to a new area. However, the job was much, much more than the job description, which is often the case. Not only did you have to care for the witness and their family's well-being, you had to safely coordinate their transportation, logistics, and security. More often you ended up dealing with prosecutors and private attorneys on a wide variety of issues that were very sensitive and not known to the public. Besides dealing with witnesses, inspectors were also called on to perform other protective operations.

When I joined Wit/Sec, the division had just been reorganized by Howard Safir. The Wit/Sec offices around the country were no longer under the chain of command of the local U.S. Marshals. The Wit/Sec Division in Headquarters was in charge of the field offices. This kept local politics of each district out of the business of the security of protecting federal witnesses. The position also required the inspector to be knowledgeable about Program guidelines. We also had to keep up to date on changes in the law. Interviewing prospective applicants for the Program would entail many, many questions concerning life-changing decisions. We needed to know answers or find out before these concerned witnesses and family members could make a decision about joining the Program, which is strictly voluntary. These people were making life-and-death decisions.

The position of inspector was supervisory when certain protective details were established. Whenever additional manpower was needed for our operations in New York, requests were made for out-of-town or local deputies from the metropolitan area to be assigned to the details. Since we were working for Headquarters, that meant our duties were twofold. We would be expected to be available to travel for protective operations worldwide and we would be expected to protect the witnesses in the Program.

Everything went along just as XXX told me it would. A teletype came out nationwide announcing XXX and I had been selected for the Witness Security inspector positions at New York Metro. Neither XXX nor XXX could imagine how my dream had come true. There was no question that working in Wit/Sec was what I wanted from the beginning when I was hired. I had anticipated that I would have to do my time at the bottom.

Everyone in the office was fair, and I got along well. I understood that I would have to attend Wit/Sec basic school and a protective operations school in Glynco, Georgia. I would also have to pass a top-secret security clearance. This was a very sensitive positon in one of the most secret government Programs. Later, I would learn that some personnel who didn't have issues with their official duties but had personal problems like poor credit, problems with their neighbors, inappropriate behavior, legal issues, criminal association, etc. had their top-secret clearances revoked until the issues were cleared. I learned early that you had to keep your nose clean both on and off the job.

I was very surprised when XXX called XXX, another Wit/Sec inspector, and me into his office and shut the door. He told us that we had been selected, along with XXX from our New York office, to participate in a major assignment. No one else in the office was aware of it—not even the office supervisor, XXX. We were instructed not to talk to anyone, even other office personnel, about the assignment. It was being planned at Headquarters and would take place within the next few weeks. As yet there was no date set, but we would be informed about a briefing shortly. The only thing on my mind was that Elaine was expecting our second child within the next few weeks. Like Catherine's birth, was I going to miss the birth of our second baby?

The following week there was a briefing by personnel from Headquarters. We were going to participate in the secret United States-East German spy exchange. The exchange was to take place on the Glienicke Bridge in Berlin, Germany. There were a couple of East German spies who had been arrested in the U.S. and were in federal prison here. XXX and I drove up to Lake Placid, New York, to pick up one of the spies. They were to be exchanged for U.S. personnel being held by the East Germans. The German spies were moved to Ft. Dix, New Jersey, and flown to Germany, where the exchange happened without incident. More importantly, the day after I was able to be with Elaine for the birth of our second daughter, Theresa Marietta. Now we had two beautiful girls. I nicknamed them G1 and G2. I took leave for the following week, knowing that I would have to go to another school in Georgia for a few weeks.

After I returned from school, my first assignment was memorable. XXX told me I was going with Inspector XXX to interview an applicant for the Program. XXX told me, "Don't develop any bad habits." XXX and I went to a hotel suite where we were to meet FBI agents and an assistant U.S. attorney to interview a witness for the Program. On the way, XXX told me he would interview the applicant and I should just sit there and observe what was going on and get an understanding of the process.

We got to the hotel and met everyone. We all sat around a large conference table in a suite. The applicant was a six-foot-five 350-pound Hells Angel. He had a full beard, the expected tattoos, and a gruff voice. When I first looked at him, I said to myself that he would be the perfect poster child for the Hells Angels.

XXX presented him with an overview of the Program and Program guidelines. After a few topics the applicant said, "I want to bring my red truck with me into the Program."

XXX informed him that he couldn't do that. It was against the rules of the Program and it was a security breach. XXX moved on to another topic. The applicant was very quiet. After a few minutes, he interrupted XXX and said again more forcefully, "I want to bring my red truck with me!"

Again XXX informed him that was against Program policy. The AUSA and the other agents also informed the applicant that it would not be possible to bring his truck. It would be a breach of his security because the truck could be traced. XXX continued explaining the Program when the applicant stood up, grabbed the table, picked it up, dropped it, and yelled, "I want to take my truck with me!"

The AUSA and the agents tried to calm him down and reassure him that he could make other plans. This huge biker was standing up towering over us and XXX said to him, "You can't take your little red wagon with you."

Now the Hells Angel was raging mad and pointed to me sitting at the other end of the table. He said, "I know why he's here."

XXX responded, "Why?"

The biker said, "He is the psychiatrist and he is watching and analyzing everything I say and do."

XXX told him, "You are right and he is not impressed."

From that day on I had a new nickname within the Marshals: "The Doctor."

In December 1985, a week before Christmas, I was sent out to Kansas City. XXX was testifying in a trial in Federal Court about corruption in the Teamsters Union. At the time XXX was one of the highest-ranking mobsters to enter the Program and was a big news item. I was assigned to the night shift in the hotel command post in the room next to where XXX was staying. After a few days of testifying, XXX was complaining of not getting dental work done in his relocation area. He wanted to go to Wit/Sec Headquarters in Washington, D.C. and talk to XXX, who handled his case. After he completed his testimony, our detail changed our plans and we ended up taking him to D.C. I was able to get home Christmas Eve. XXX passed away in 1992 from Alzheimer's disease and a stroke.

In April 1986, XXX and I had another assignment to go get XXX, a mob prisoner witness who was incarcerated. He was out in a hole in a desolate local jail in the middle of the desert in Arizona. We were to bring him back to New York. When we got to Arizona, we rented a Lincoln Town Car, knowing we would be doing long highway driving. The next day we went out and picked up XXX. The jail was a few hours from the airport. I was driving and we were cruising along, way above the speed limit. We couldn't see any cars for miles. I asked XXX if he knew the color of police lights in Arizona. He said blue. I asked him to look in his side mirror because there had been a faint blue light miles behind us for a while. He suggested I slow down. There were no other cars on the road. The blue flashing light started getting bigger and bigger. Finally I could see an old pickup truck with a blue light on the dash. We could see that the driver was a very large officer wearing a cowboy hat who just about filled up the whole front cabin of the truck. I thought of Jonathan Winters driving the truck in the movie *It's a Mad, Mad, Mad, Mad World*. Somehow, though, I didn't think this would be as funny.

I slowed down and pulled over. The officer got out, wearing a pearl handle six-shooter on his hip. He was not happy. We ID'd ourselves and he looked in the back and saw XXX handcuffed. He said, "Damn it! I have been chasing you for miles. You know you are going through an Indian reservation? I called ahead, so there is a roadblock up ahead to stop you. I will call them, but be safe and have a good day."

We got moving again and a few miles ahead there were two Bureau of Indian Affairs police cars parked on the side of the road. As we passed, we beeped and they waved. XXX told XXX to "watch out the window and let us know if you see any Indians."

XXX said he knew he would someday end up in jail but never thought he would be driving with two crazy marshals looking for Indians in Arizona! He said, "Just get me back to Brooklyn alive."

In May 1986, I had to attend another training school for Protection and Personal Security. That was for a couple of weeks in Georgia. The Judicial Security Division also sent their personnel to that school. It consisted mostly of physical training, tactics, and weapons qualifications, high-speed driving and evasive techniques. My friend Bill Fitzgerald had transferred into Judicial Security, which provides security for federal judges and Supreme Court justices. Bill and I drove down to Georgia and roomed together for the school. Bill was a former Fordham University grad and U.S. Army Ranger. He had been shot up in Vietnam and had problems with one leg because of war injuries. There was a final physical training test with a required time to complete a mile-and-a-half run. I had trained with Bill to make the run. If you washed out, you couldn't keep your position. Bill had been training hard and knew what he had to do. To this day I give Bill credit for making the run and graduating. Through determination, sense of purpose, and true grit, he had succeeded where some others had not. There is no question that military training and a fearless drive helped him.

July 4, 1986 was the 100th celebration of the Statue of Liberty. NY Metro supported the Judicial Security Division for the security detail for the weekend activities. Chief Justice of the Supreme Court Warren Berger and his wife would be under our protection for "Liberty Weekend." The chief justice would be attending most of the events and swearing in new citizens on Ellis Island for the celebration. Dave Neff was the agent in charge (AIC). He came in from Colorado to run the detail. It was a full detail with NYPD lead cars with Intel and Special Operations support. I was assigned as the limo driver for the chief justice and his wife. Neff was in the front seat with me. When the chief justice arrived for the first time at JFK Airport, it was a long ride into Manhattan, but not because of traffic. With NYPD leading with lights and sirens, we buzzed right through traffic and into Manhattan. The chief justice did not like all the security. He kept asking Dave why there was so much security, and why did the NYPD have to use their lights and sirens to get us through the traffic? Mrs. Berger would say, "Oh, that's all right, dear." Dave and I rolled our eyes a few times, thinking this was going to be a long weekend.

We arrived at the Waldorf Towers, where the Bergers would be guests for the weekend. Because of the events most streets were shut down. We had authorization from Headquarters to be housed in the city for the weekend. Around the Waldorf it was very busy and congested, with many celebrities in town for the events. At the time Frank Sinatra had an apartment in the Towers. We would see him and other celebs coming and going all day. The doorman showed us a plaque on the side of the building recognizing General MacArthur, who had lived there for a period. His wife was still residing there and would enter and leave by wheelchair with an attendant. She was very pleasant and we would welcome her every morning. A few months later I happened to be walking past the Towers and saw Mrs. MacArthur being wheeled down the sidewalk. I said, "Good afternoon, Mrs. MacArthur." As I walked past I could hear her say to her aide, "How did he know me?"

During that "Liberty Weekend" we made trips around the city, and the chief justice became more relaxed and enjoyed the events. We went to St. Patrick's for a special Mass with Cardinal O'Conner. The chief justice was invited to watch the fireworks from a law firm at 20 Exchange Place near Wall Street that looks out on the harbor and the Statue of Liberty. At first, he didn't want to attend. His wife had to talk him into it. She told him it would be nice for their staff and the security personnel to see the fireworks. The chief justice gave in and said okay.

Most of the avenues and streets were shut down and overcrowded with people everywhere. We slowly made our way downtown and got to the building. Part of the security detail brought the chief justice and his wife upstairs to the law firm that invited him to watch the display. We found out there was an outdoor rooftop to the building where you could see the statue. I asked Dave if I could go up because I had brought my camera and was hoping to get some amazing photos. He said okay but to keep my radio on. XXX, another inspector from NY Metro, also brought her camera, so we went up together. It was crowded but we had a great location and took shots of the fireworks and the Statue of Liberty. Halfway through the fireworks, the chief justice decided to leave. Dave called me on the radio to let us know. We had to get an elevator to get down, and they were slow and packed with people. I called Dave and told him we were on our way but the elevators were slow. I could hear other transmissions of the motorcade leaving. Just as we got past the front door and out on the street, I heard Dave say the motorcade was moving slowly through the traffic. XXX and I could see the follow car at the end of the motorcade crawling through the crowds. We started running after the follow car and caught up to it. Standard operating procedures were for the follow car to have windows down and armed agents in the back sitting sideways, looking out to neutralize any threat. I ran up along the follow car and the guy in the rear said, "What the hell are you doing here? Aren't you supposed to be driving the limo?" We jumped in the follow car. Just then NYPD cleared the street and the motorcade picked up speed and we headed back uptown to the Waldorf. By the end of the detail, the chief justice and his wife were very pleasant. On the day of their departure, they presented all of us with autographed copies of a book on the history of the Supreme Court.

In March 1987, I flew to Atlanta to assist in the court appearance production of XXX, a Colombian drug kingpin. XXX was cooperating but was incarcerated in the federal pen in Atlanta, Georgia. I met up with XXX, chief of the Miami region, and some other out-of-town inspectors. We took XXX by a small U.S. Coast Guard jet to Florida for a court appearance. The next day we put a bulletproof vest and black jacket on him for his court appearance. After the production,

XXX told me to rent a van and take all the other out-of-town inspectors to the airport for their flights home, and then for me to turn in the van and go back to New York. After I dropped everyone off, I turned the van into the rental returns area. As I was walking past the van, I looked inside to make sure no one had left anything. To my surprise there was a briefcase and the black jacket. As soon as I saw the briefcase, I knew what was in it. It was a specially built case to hold an Uzi sub-machine gun. I opened the case to make sure it was in there with the additional clips and ammo. It was. I took the black jacket and stuffed it into my luggage. I had about thirty minutes to catch my flight, which I was not going to miss.

Carrying my bag and briefcase, I checked in for my flight. This was pre-9/11 and I followed all the requirements for armed agents to fly. On the form that I had to fill out, it indicated where I was seated on the plane. I was carrying my own weapon anyway, and no one at the security checkpoint opened up the briefcase I was carrying. That was normal. A local police officer had to come to the security checkpoint to verify my credentials as an armed agent. The stewardess and the airline captain knew where I was sitting. That was standard procedure in case of an emergency. After I boarded the plane awaiting takeoff, I observed the stewardess walking up the aisle toward where I was sitting. I could tell she was looking for me because she was holding a copy of the firearm boarding form in her hand. I was sitting in an aisle seat. She whispered in my ear that the airline received a call from the local office that I had something that belonged to them. Someone was on their way to meet me at the gate. The stewardess said she could give the item to the gate agent. I said no. I would wait at the gate for them, but I was not going to miss the flight. I told her not to leave without me and to let me know one minute before she closed the door. I waited, no one showed, so I got back on the plane.

That evening when I got back to New York, I called XXX to advise him. He had already received a call from XXX. He was upset that I kept the Uzi. XXX told him that I saved someone from getting time on the street or fired. Miami wanted New York to know that the Uzi was on Miami inventory and wanted it back. Eventually we arranged to get the Uzi back to Miami. We didn't need it. We had a few of our own.

XXX, an executive of a garbage company in New Jersey, became an informant for the FBI in the late 1970s and 1980s. He voluntarily came forward to wear a wire for the FBI because he strongly objected to the involvement of organized crime in the dumping of toxic waste. XXX testified in numerous trials and organized crime State and Federal Commission hearings. Physically, XXX was a small man with a squeaky voice who reminded me of Truman Capote. One day XXX and I escorted XXX, who was not in custody, to testify in a hearing. Afterward we were taking him to a local New York airport. We were stuck in traffic and XXX, who was sitting in the backseat, was whining and complaining about everything. Inspector XXX, who is tall with long arms and legs, reached over the front seat and grabbed XXX by his tie and yanked him up to the front seat. I was driving and turned my head to my right. I could see XXX's bright red face with bulging eyes on top of the front bench seat. He was trying to scream but he sounded like Bugs Bunny! XXX told him, "Shut up, you little weasel, you are making me sick!" With that he pushed him back into his seat. XXX was kicking and screaming, "I am going to tell Howard Safir!"

Evidently, he did lodge a complaint against Inspector XXX because a few weeks later, XXX told me that he had received a letter from Wit/Sec Headquarters forbidding him to have any further contact with XXX. He said, "Oh, how disappointing!" Sometime after that a TV movie was made called *A Deadly Business* starring Alan

Arkin as XXX. I doubt the car scene made it into the movies.

Over the years I am sure the budget for the Program has grown. I never followed what the yearly budget was to operate the Program. However, when a witness in the Program testifies in open court, the defense attorneys usually request from the Program how much money the Government has spent on the witness and the family. I have turned over many financial reports to defense attorneys who had to sign an acknowledgment of possessing the information. Of course, the normal stage would be set for the defense attorneys carrying the documents to approach a witness on the stand in front of a jury and to ask the witness if it is true that the government has spent a specified amount of taxpayers' money to relocate him and his family. The witness would have no idea how much that amount is. The witness only would know how much money they received as a monthly stipend for a certain period of time. When a witness enters the Program, they do not sign a contract that says they will be paid X amount of money for testifying. They sign a Memorandum of Understanding that spells out what is expected from them and what they can expect from the government. The costs involved with relocating a witness vary by location, family size, and what types of services are needed. It doesn't matter what the status of the applicant is. The boss of a crime family would be paid the same as a local street drug dealer. Of course, the amount is determined by the cost of living in their relocation area. The Program follows the numbers provided by the Bureau of Labor Statistics for the cost of living in a geographical area.

When people found out that I worked in the Program, they would ask me if I ever met XXX of *Goodfellas* movie fame. Actually, I had. I dealt with XXX a few times over the years. He was quite the character, always pushing the envelope. He was an easy one to size up. He wasn't going to change, no way. One time he was in New York to testify in a case. After he completed his testimony, Inspector XXX and I took him to a New York area airport. While we were walking to the gate, XXX took out a marijuana cigarette and lit it up. I told him to put it out and toss it in the can, which he did, but only after he took a few more drags. He always thought he was getting over on us by bringing bottles of booze with him whenever he came to New York to testify, hiding the bottles in the drop ceiling where he was staying. The chief inspector would yell and scream at him, and XXX would tell him where to go. When he was in town, you never knew what he was going to do next. He was just one of those witnesses who never was going to change his ways. He failed to take advantage of a new life and continued to swim in turbulent waters. His main criminal case was the high-profile XXX at XXX. Many people associated with XXX were found murdered. AUSA Ed McDonald, who was the prosecutor, saved XXX's life by having him brought in and arrested. In his old life, XXX was marked for death. He finally cooperated with us. He had drug problems as well as other issues. He was always nervous and could not adjust to a quiet life in the shadows. It is not unusual for some of these characters to want to capitalize on their fame. After he was relocated numerous times in different relocation areas, he was terminated from the Program for various violations. Over the years, he wound up with a multitude of arrests for crimes in different areas of the country. He passed away in a hospital in XXX.

Not all cooperating witnesses who testify for the government and enter Wit/Sec World are "bent-nosed" Mafioso men. We have had more than a few women. There was one unforgettable female witness we were handling who was involved in a drug case. She was attractive and would stand out in a crowd like a Playboy model. Her name was XXX. If I remember correctly she was a singer in a nightclub in New York. A drug dealer started having a relationship with her, and she moved into his "mini mansion" in an exclusive neighborhood in Westchester. The Drug Enforcement Agency (DEA) had the location under surveillance. One day when she was leaving the residence, the agents followed her and then stopped her. They made their pitch, and she decided to cooperate. She never returned to the house. At the time, Westchester County needed her to testify in one of their cases. The ADAs assigned to the case were Jeanne Pirro and Janet DeFiore. I advised them to tell XXX to tone it down a little. We would never want witnesses to bring unwanted attention to themselves in public. She would show up at the airport decked out with a white fur coat, short skirt, and high heel boots. She turned heads. Her arrival was never discreet, but dealing with her was more enjoyable than dealing with some of the other cooperators!

In April 1987, the NY Metro Office was tasked with a protective detail on Armando Fernandez Larios. This was one of those "special cases." Fernandez was a major in the Chilean Army. He was an agent for the Chilean secret police and had knowledge of the 1976 car bombing in the Washington, D.C. area of the former Chilean ambassador to the U.S., Orlando Letelier. This unfortunate event also killed an American, Ronni Moffitt, who was in the car with Letelier. The bombing was related to Chilean politics. Letelier was a political opponent of Chilean dictator General Augusto Pinochet.

We kept Fernandez at a safe house under twenty-four-hour protection in the New York area. It was a very unusual situation because his wife and private attorney were authorized to visit Fernandez, who was not in custody at that time. When they visited from Washington, D.C., they brought wine, food, candles, tablecloths—all the comforts not usually provided at a government safe house.

That detail lasted a few months. Every so often we would take him out and around the city to sightsee just for a change of scenery. Once we took him to the upper West Side to visit President Grant's tomb because he enjoyed military history. When it was time for him to leave, after many months, Fernandez gave the office a very moving letter about how at first he did not know what to expect and how now he felt like he was leaving his family. *The Washington Post* on May 7, 1988 had an article on page seven about Fernandez.

Sometimes other inspectors would ask me why we were protecting this guy or that guy. These special cases did not fit in the square peg of the Witness Protection Program. However, because at the time New York Metro and the Program had the capability, we were tasked to protect these principals. It did not matter that the case was not organized crime. Usually, these special cases involved espionage, terrorism, and foreigners. They were all short-term solutions to complex situations.

In early 1988, another special protective detail was set up for a "special case." XXX was XXX General Counsel in New York and the chief political advisor to XXX. NY Metro received a phone call from Headquarters to pick up XXX and his family and to get them out of New York ASAP. XXX and some other inspectors met XXX and his family and got them out of town. A detail was set up on XXX and his family in the Washington, D.C. area. XXX had accused XXX of XXX and corruption. I was assigned to the detail as the night shift supervisor for two weeks. XXX and his family received twenty-four-hour protection. XXX first testified in XXX hearings. Later he would testify in XXX Federal Court in the trial against XXX, who ultimately was convicted and sent to prison.

Another very unusual case in early 1988 involved two Sikh Indians who were arrested in New Jersey on terrorism charges filed in India. A former assistant U.S. attorney from the District of New Jersey, was appointed as a special prosecutor to handle the extradition hearings for the Sikhs, and she received typewritten death threats at her residence. The USMS Special Operations Group was flown into Newark to provide security around the courthouse, including the rooftop. A special twenty-four-hour security detail was provided for the prosecutor's residence. She was moved out of her apartment in New Jersey to a safe house in New York, and our office provided personal security for her traveling to and from court.

Normally, "protectees" don't mingle with the security personnel. In this case, she always wanted to sit and talk with the detail. That is not usually a good sign. Soon after, the prosecutor was approached with the results of an investigation. The typewriter in her apartment was used to create the envelopes containing the death threats that the prosecutor had fabricated herself. The U.S. attorney at the time was Sam Alito, who recused himself from prosecuting her because she had previously worked for that office. The Department of Justice in Washington prosecuted her. She pled not guilty by reason of insanity. This incident resurfaced in Judge Alito's Senate confirmation application for the Supreme Court but had no negative reflection on his appointment.

Besides amending the Witness Security Program to include families of Wit/Sec participants, the Comprehensive Crime Control Act of 1984 created a new section in the U.S. Criminal Code for Hostage Taking, and the Omnibus Diplomatic Security and Antiterrorism Act of 1986 established a new extraterritorial statute pertaining to terrorist acts conducted abroad against U.S. citizens.

In 1985, Fawaz Younis, a Lebanese hijacker, was involved in the hijacking of a Royal Jordanian plane with four Americans on board. After releasing the passengers, the hijackers blew up the plane. In 1987, Younis was lured by undercover FBI agents aboard a yacht off the coast of Cyprus in international waters and arrested in a drug sting operation. He was the first person charged under the new hostage-taking statute and brought to the U.S. to stand trial. Younis was housed at FCI Otisville, New York, while on trial in Washington, D.C. The Wit/Sec Division, with the support of our

Special Operations Group, would move Younis by helicopter from Otisville to D.C. My assignment was to make the arrangements and meet the team at Otisville on their departures and arrivals. Sometimes at the conclusion of the moves, I would provide pizza and beer for the USMS personnel. On those occasions I got to talk to members, including Bill Degan. In 1992, Bill was shot and killed in the standoff shootout incident at Ruby Ridge. Younis was convicted in his case and sentenced to thirty years in prison, and in 2005, he was deported back to Lebanon.

The Wit/Sec Division provides additional protective operations beyond their normal duties as authorized by the attorney general of the United States. Former Chief Jack Brophy was instrumental in establishing an agreement with the U.S. Department of State to assist them with security during the United Nations General Assembly (UNGA) in New York. During UNGA the State Department needs extra security personnel for protective operations for the additional foreign dignitaries who convene every fall in New York. For two years in the early 1990s, I was the USMS coordinator for that operation. During that time, I lived in the Summit Hotel on Lexington Avenue where we had our command post. I had to coordinate with the State Department the arrival of approximately fifty USMS personnel from all around the country. This included hotel rooms; briefings on policies and procedures; work schedules and approving their hours and dealing with issues that would arise. My old friend Tony Termini, from my days at Loews Hotels, was the manager of the hotel. My past affiliation with Tony was an added benefit while living and working in the hotel. I socialized with Tony and, as a result, I received invitations to Christmas parties and other events at the Summit and other NYC hotels.

During my last year there, my assistant was XXX from the Boston Office who took over command the following year. Ever since we worked together during UNGA and up to the present time, there has been a yearly golf match between the New York office and the Boston office in a neutral location. My partner for that match is XXX. Every year after the match, my partner called XXX, a former coworker and former chief of the division in Headquarters, and report the results of yet another NY victory. That brought joy to the chief! I can say without a doubt that the "curse of the Babe" still lives!

Similarly, that territorial "pride" was never an issue. It didn't matter to us in New York which investigative agency was sponsoring a witness for the Program. In very rare cases, the Marshals Service Enforcement Division also placed witnesses in the Program. The atmosphere between Wit/Sec, USMS districts, and other agencies was very cooperative. There were no disparaging remarks about other federal agencies or agents. At times, I had to remind myself of the original intent of the Wit/Sec Program. We were fighting the war against organized crime. It was a team effort in keeping people safe and secure in order for them to testify. In New York Metro, we had a good relationship with the many prosecutors and agents from the different agencies in the area. To this day, I still keep in touch with judges, prosecutors, agents, and marshals I worked with over thirty years ago.

5

Family Secrets

"It's wishful thinking. I think everybody would like to have somebody that they could go to for justice, without going through the law courts and the lawyers. The Godfather *was really, to me, a family novel, more than a crime novel."*

—Mario Puzo

One of the most difficult areas of concern for families entering the Program is establishing a cover story of their past while attempting to adjust to their new life in a new area. The United States has a very large mobile and transient community. Currently it has become more common for someone from New York or any major city to move into Any Town, USA. Our world has gotten smaller and less private. The younger generation of today is so active on social networks that they are constantly telling family and friends everything they do or say, and everywhere they go. That also includes sending and receiving photographs online. Even taking pictures of the food they are eating! Will they ever be able to maintain family secrets?

When Program members enter WitSec World, sometimes they have to divulge information about their families that they never would have had to if they were not in the situation in which they now found themselves. This hidden information is not only shared with the government but also with psychiatrists. In my opinion, one of the reasons that *The Sopranos* was a successful TV show was that David Chase, the man behind the series, created this middle-aged man who had problems in his relationship with his wife and kids. He also visited a psychiatrist, and oh, by the way, he just happened to be a mob boss. That was a new spin on mob life. In the real world if you are coming into the Program, you are going to see a psychiatrist.

These secrets have caused a strain on the relationships within families in the Program and with relatives not in the Program. Program participants are not supposed to tell anyone—including their non-Program relatives, U.S. attorneys, or agents—their new names, locations, or phone numbers. The consequences can be deadly.

There are many communities throughout the U.S. with very friendly citizens; with Welcome Wagons to greet new members of a given community; with neighbors who just want to know because they like to make connections. All this "shooting the breeze," to use an old saying, may be fine for most, but for these newly relocated families, it can escalate their stress factor, especially if they do not have a strong backstory. Some members end up breaching their own security by talking too much. As you can imagine, this is not easy for some families. Parents living in WitSec World can usually stay glued to their story. Many times, it becomes a problem with minor children who were born and then relocated with their parents. It is less of a problem with children born in the relocation area. Those children grow up only knowing Wit/Sec World. It is up to the parents to decide if they ever want to expose those children to their family secret about their past life.

I have had conversations with Program parents who want to

successfully don their new clothes and embrace life in the new area, but despite their best efforts, they still feel out of place and awkward. They may still look over their shoulder. It is not an authentic life. They feel it is a life of lies. As a result, they have a very difficult time adjusting. Program participants go through counseling in their relocation area to address this and other major issues to assist them in their relocation process.

I have been impressed with the maturity of some of the young adults who have sat in on preliminary interviews as applicants for the Program. Some of them were also with their parents or guardian and had to be interviewed. Some parents did not take their children with them into the Program. There were many different scenarios. Every family is different and every case is different. Occasionally, primary witnesses will not uproot their families because the adjustment is extremely demanding and difficult. Some primary witnesses leave their whole family back in the old area because they do not want to put them through the difficult adjustment of the Program. This type of decision making would depend on the threat assessment against the family. Sometimes after the primary witness is relocated and time goes by, the family reunites.

This Program is the "Program of Last Resort." While not everyone who testifies against the mob will need the Program, for those who do, the Program is available and it is voluntary. Some don't take it and make other choices. In the U.S. Attorney's Manual for the application process, the prosecutors have to answer if they explored all other options for the witness before they can apply for the Program.

One of the greatest freedoms of living in the U.S. is that every citizen has the freedom of choice. However, for citizens living the life of the mob, their freedom of choice was often limited to either jail or death. In essence, they gave up their freedom of choice. While living "the life" they were swimming in turbulent waters, riding rough waves. There were always highs and lows, ups and downs. There was always the worry of never knowing where they would end up and never knowing if their best friend would be the one who gets the orders to put a bullet in the back of their head. Their being in "the life" had taken away their freedom to choose. Those who were fortunate to make the choice felt there was no other way out but the Program.

After the Program was created, the government threw those who wanted a different choice a way out—a life preserver to put around their necks. The name of that life preserver is the Witness Security Program. Some clung tightly and never looked back. However, some who hung on to that life preserver never grasped it fully. Some let go and swam on their own; others didn't make it and ended up drowning.

Some witnesses leave the Program and return to the old area. This can be for numerous personal reasons: they can't make it in their relocation area; the rules and regulations are too restrictive; they miss the neighborhood, family, and friends; or there is no longer a threat. Some unofficially bring their unauthorized mistresses into the relocation area, which could result in termination from the Program.

Some large-scale drug cases include relocating extended families from overseas. However, some cases are not as sophisticated, and witnesses who testify in these cases don't need the Program. They may only need to leave the Bronx, for example, and move to Long Island, upstate, or New Jersey to live happily ever after. Every case and area is different. For a while there was a short-term relocation Program to deal with the drug gangs in the Washington, D.C. area. Depending on the gangs and threat assessments, the witnesses who testified in those gangbanging cases were relocated in the Program but only received limited services for a short period of time. It was enough to rescue them from those turbulent waters in the storm.

One of the first steps in the application process is the interview to collect information about the applicant. That information, along with a threat assessment and other material, is forwarded to Wit/Sec Headquarters, where decisions are made about the case. When I interviewed XXX for the Program, his teenage daughter was one of the family members present. She was very mature for a young teenager and understood some of the information I presented better than her father. She spoke good English. Sometimes she would politely ask questions without first consulting her father and then explain my answers to him. Although there was an Italian interpreter present, XXX would ask her questions and she would clarify issues with me. At one point I looked into XXX's eyes and could see he was very proud of her.

Another young adult who was very helpful to his father was XXX's teenage son. The father was a capo in the XXX family. I never personally interviewed him for the Program. However, after XXX was shot in an assassination attempt on his life at a XXX, he decided to cooperate, and entered the Program to later return to New York many times to testify and for other court productions. His son and sometimes XXX would accompany him to assist him with his personal hygiene and other matters. Even after he got out of the hospital after recuperating from the attempt on his life, he still had physical issues.

Some young adults would cause unintended security concerns for their relocated family. For example, the teenage son of a particular relocated family was an exceptional football player. When they got settled in their new area, the son went out for the new local high school sports team. Not only did he make the team, he became a superstar. The local newspapers started asking where this new player came from. This is exactly the type of attention the family does not want. Yes, the family grabbed the life preserver and diligently started a "straight" life, but it comes with a cost that they could never have imagined—you don't know until you know. Sometimes Program members and, unfortunately, Program children cannot continue with their interests in their new areas because it brings too much attention to their assimilation process and could end up being a breach of their security.

Communicating in society has changed and communicating among family members has also changed. Maintaining family secrets may also be changing. In our new world of social media, with everything being instantaneous on YouTube and in the news, most new events become live for the whole world to witness. Our personal lives are now an open book. These new media sites can be a concern for Program participants.

When I first started working, pagers and beepers were concerns for relocated witnesses because they could reveal locations. Then caller ID appeared; then the cell phone. Today social media networks and other technological advances that may or may not be good for society are definitely a security concern for the Program. The Program has adjusted by staying ahead of the curve. I hope it continues to be successful at any cost.

I have personally experienced dealing with family secrets. Over the years I would take my elderly mother to her family cemetery plot to visit, bring flowers, clean up, and just sit and talk. The large plot has space to bury ten people. The tombstone is a large Vermont granite stone slab with the names of the deceased and a large angel statue above the slab looking over the plot, standing guard. One day while I was there with my mother, I was looking at the names and noticed one name with the letters GMO. I asked her who that was and she stated that was her uncle Giacomo. The dates were from 1889–1919. I had never heard of him and wondered why he had only lived to be thirty. I wasn't much older, so I asked her what happened to him. She said no one in the family ever knew what happened to him. I didn't say anything. As time went by and I revisited the cemetery, I would think about who this person was and what happened to him. I wrote down his name and date of death. Months later I went to the local library and scanned the newspaper on that date. I came across a headline: "TWO FORMER RESIDENTS MURDERED IN NEW YORK." I read the article in disbelief. "Two men were killed and a third mortally wounded in a gun battle during which 40 shots were fired at Catherine and Madison Streets on the lower east side of New York City. The dead are Giacomo Graziano, 30, No. 74 Oliver Street and Louis Valenti 38, No. 78 Catherine Street." The article went on to say four men were arrested at the scene. I didn't say anything to anyone for months. One day at a family function, I approached my mother's brother Lee and asked him if he ever knew what happened to Giacomo. He said no he didn't. I attempted to show him the article, but he wouldn't even look at it. He said, "Come on; let's take a walk." He said he never told anyone this, but when he was younger, his father took him to a walk-up tenement building in lower Manhattan. His father knocked on a door and a man opened the door and put his hands up and started walking backward. His father said to the man, "Don't worry. I am not going to harm you. Put your hands down. I just came here to introduce you to my son. I wanted him to meet the man who killed his uncle." They all had a shot of whiskey and then Uncle Lee and his father left. Uncle Lee said he never knew why Giacomo was killed or whatever happened to the guy he met in that building with his father. He said it may have been a mistaken identity.

No one in the family ever talked about it, Uncle Lee never mentioned it again, and neither did I. I never mentioned it to my mother. My uncle Lee passed away in the late 1990s. After I retired, my mother passed away. I suspect there was more to the story, but I would not disturb those whom I thought might know. Why? If at any time when they were alive and wanted to tell, they would have. I learned to respect their silence. They took that family secret and maybe more to their grave. So, I let it rest with them.

But my curiosity was piqued. I wanted the details. When I first found out about this family secret in the late 1980s, there was always that curiosity in the back of my mind to find out all the details, facts, and where they might lead. My dilemma was: do I dig deeper into this incident to find out the truth? Was Giacomo shot and killed by mistake? If not, then why? These were my relatives. Were they involved in illegal activities? Also, this didn't just happen, and the facts may not be fresh in people's minds. It was almost a hundred years ago! Was any information passed down to anyone? Family secrets sometimes get convoluted from hearsay and myths. The only truths are those from eyewitnesses and participants of the stories. And that is only when they want to be willing and forthright. Sometimes, time removes the truths and you get watered-down versions of the events, misinformation, exaggerated truths, or even outright lies. I know about lies. Working in law enforcement I was used to being lied to. Hearsay is not admissible. So, whenever I would hear family or friends talking about "old family stories," I would be very skeptical if the people talking were not present at the incidents mentioned. I have to remember that I am writing my memoir. This book is about my experiences in life that I am passing on. However, that thick block of granite of a headstone held another family tragedy.

There was another name on that gravestone across from Giacomo that caught my attention and became a new focus. It was Josephine Graziano (1905–1922), seventeen years old at her death! I had asked my mother about her. She was more open and saddened by Josephine's passing. When my mother emigrated from Sicily, she came with her mother, sister Rosie, brother Lee, and her oldest sister Josephine. Josephine was sixteen years old at the time. Josephine had her own passport photo in my grandmother's passport along with the other children. That passport and photos have since been passed down to me.

My mother told me that prior to leaving Sicily, a young boy Josephine's age was in love with her. He lived on a nearby farm. His family and he did not want Josephine to leave for America. They begged her and her mother not to leave Sicily. They wanted Josephine to stay with the boyfriend's family. My grandparents objected and Josephine departed with her family for the long journey, never to return.

After my grandparents and their family settled in Highland Falls, New York, Josephine was hired at the laundry at nearby West Point. On her first day of work, she was dressed in a pretty new dress and new shoes. My mother's version of the following incident was that Josephine was not familiar with an elevator in the building. She opened the door and fell into the elevator trap. The elevator came down and crushed her to death. That was also the family story from my other aunts and uncles. Out of curiosity, I again went to the local library and retrieved a copy of the news of her death in the 1922 edition of the local paper, which read, "Death of Miss Graziano." The article describes "the injuries to her body being remarkable considering the short distance she fell. There was a dislocation of the neck, a gash extending in the jaw and requiring several stitches to close and one of the ears was partially severed." The article also reads that "the authorities said it would have been impossible for the elevator to cause the injuries because there are bumpers on the bottom of the elevator." The article referred to "the funeral which had a large clock made out of flowers with the hands indicating the time of her death."

Only a few years ago, Dolly Vanzetta, whose family owned a grocery store in the Italian section of town, told my wife Elaine that she remembered her family talking about the incident. She stated that Josephine was "hit and pushed down that shaft by a girl who was jealous of Josephine. The girl liked a boy, but the boy liked Josephine. A love triangle! There was something not right with the girl." That was all she would say. Josephine survived that long, hard trip from Sicily only to meet her death at the hands of a lovesick, deranged girl on her first day at work. How unbelievably sad is that!

When I searched for the information about what happened to Giacomo and Josephine, I felt I was exploring an archeological dig. However, this was not a dig into the earth of that cemetery plot; it was a dig into family souls and secrets. When I questioned my mother and my uncle Lee about these events, my goal was not just information. I had that already in black-and-white news. I wanted to hear their story and feel their emotions. It is their feelings over facts. Memory has its own story. Thinking back to these family secrets and other events in my life, I learned that I can only tell stories that are in my head. I can only put into words what my memory tells me. My life becomes evidence. On these pages are my memories only.

I looked back at these incidents and thought they were all part of the evolution of an immigrant family assimilating into the American society at that time. Were there other incidents related to these deaths that were not shared and passed on to the family? Nothing could be worse than the killing of a family member. They were different times, with different people experiencing a new life in what was then a new world. Just as today it is different, with the young people learning to survive in a new, modern, global, wireless world and experiencing new things. It is also the same with people in the Program being relocated to a new location, starting over again, assimilating into society with their own family secrets.

6

The Sicilians

"He who doesn't fear death dies only once."
—Judge Giovanni Falcone

The history of the Sicilian Mafia has been well documented in books, movies, and on television. My story is not intended to repeat the history of those events of the past. However, I would like you, the reader, to understand what I consider to be an important part of the war against organized crime: the people who cooperated with the government. I consider myself to be fortunate to have participated in a small way working for the government at a crucial period in that war. The part I am describing is the role that the cooperating witnesses played for the first time against the mob. For centuries, organized crime operated by killing people who cooperated and talked to the authorities. This put fear in all men who took their oath of silence. In the United States the creation of the Witness Protection Program gave members of La Costa Nostra a new option. For the first time, they felt they could break their code of silence and feel confident that they and their family could live safely in a new area with a new identity in the Program. As a result, the foundations of these criminal groups started crumbling. Over the years, the success of the Program spread around the world as other countries studied our Program and we assisted them in starting their own.

For centuries, landowners in Sicily set up private little armies of their own to defend their families and estates from marauding bandits. The so-called *compagnie d'arni* maintained some sort of primitive justice by drastic means: as they had no courts of law and no prisons, they had to punish the smallest crime with the death sentence. Justice was conceived as something innate in man; wrongs were righted, the weak defended, robbers punished, the outraged virgins married off to the seducers, according to what was, in reality, a rough peasant version of the code of chivalry which the Norman invaders had brought to the island in 1070, and which had been kept alive by the *teatro dei pupi*, the puppets' theatre, frequented by grownups as well as children, dedicated to the noble feats of Charlemagne's knights.

In the Sicilian Mafia, there are cliques within their families called "cosche." *Cosca* etymologically refers to artichoke (Italian: *carciofo*; Sicilian: *cacocciula*), especially the hardest parts of the leaves. The closely folded and spiny leaves very clearly symbolize the tightly knit and fearsome features of the cosca. A feud that cost hundreds of lives almost a century ago, between the *stoppaglieri cosca* of Monreale and the *fratuzzi* of Bagheria, is still remembered. One of the fratuzzi, Salvatore d'Amico, who had lost all his family, at one point turned informer. He told the police all he knew and then said: "I shall die killed by the Mafia. Neither you nor all the police in the Kingdom of Italy will be able to save me."

Eleven days later he was found riddled with bullets, with a cork in his mouth, the symbol of the stoppaglieri, and an image of the Madonna del Carmine, the symbol of the fratuzzi, on his chest. The two fighting cosche had forgotten their enmity for the time strictly necessary to punish him. He had committed the ultimate crime for all Mafia men; he had talked to the authorities. D'Amico was one of the earliest of the Sicilian Mafia to cooperate with the police and be killed for it.

Legendary and still revered above all in Sicily is the name of the late Don Vito Cascio Ferro, perhaps the greatest the Mafia ever had, who reigned from the end of the 1890s till the late twenties. In 1900 he came to America and soon became one of the major exponents of the Mano Nera (Black Hand). He was expelled from the United States. Back in Sicily, he resumed his ordinary criminal activities with old and new affiliates.

He admitted having killed one man in his long life, only one, and not for money, but for the honor, prestige, and preservation of the society. The man had challenged the Mafia as a whole and had to be killed personally by Don Vito and nobody else. He was Giuseppe Petrosino, the head of the Italian squad of the New York City Police Department who had come to Palermo in 1909 to study the Mafia and Cascio Ferro's criminal career. Petrosino was not Sicilian and did not know the Sicilian ways. He was from Padula, in the province of Salerno, and immigrated to the United States in 1873, when he was thirteen years old. He thought he was safe, as nobody knew of his arrival except the police. Don Vito shot him a few hours after his landing, in the street, in the Piazza Marina, in front of the courthouse. Don Vito was arrested in 1926 for the first and only time. He was tried inconclusively sixty-nine times before. He was sentenced to a prison term for the murder.

Mussolini vowed to smash the Honorable Society once and for all. The dictator chose a northern official, Cesare Mori, as commander of his anti-Mafia offensive and gave him strong police forces and sweeping powers. Mori had thousands of suspects rounded up and interned or exiled without trial. Il Duce also proclaimed he had rooted out the Sicilian Mafia. It would only lie low for a few years.[4]

Lt. Giuseppe Petrosino lived in New York across the street from Kenmare Square Park at Lafayette Street and Cleveland Place. In 1895, he was made sergeant upon Police Commissioner Teddy Roosevelt's recommendation. He always wore his signature derby and was called the "Detective in the Derby." After he made lieutenant, he was put in command of the Italian Legion, organized specifically to combat organized crime. Some five hundred gangsters were reputedly jailed through the legion's work. After Petrosino was shot and killed in Palermo, his body was brought back to New York. His funeral procession in Little Italy, led by a hearse drawn by six horses, was attended by 250,000 people, according to Dr. Emelise Aleandri. Kenmare Square Park across from his home was renamed Petrosino Park. The leadership of the Italian squad went to "Treat 'em Rough" Mike Fiaschetti, who reportedly sent a hundred men to the electric chair.[5]

In Palermo there are memorials on the streets in honor of the Italian anti-mafia police and prosecutors killed in the line of duty. One evening while in Palermo, I was walking past one of those memorials. I took a picture of the stone block dedicated to the work of Calogero Zucchetto and thought about his career. He had been a member of the anti-Mafia police of the Polizia di Stato. A major Mafia war was going on. At the time, Zucchetto was searching for the Mafia boss, Salvatore Montalto. He had information from Sicilian Mafia member XXX, who was a cooperator. Later, XXX became a witness whom we handled during the Pizza Trial in New York.

On the evening of November 14, 1982, Zucchetto, twenty-seven years old, was leaving a bar in Palermo. He was killed by two men on a motorcycle who put five bullets in his head. On the plaque it is written that he was assassinated by the hand of the Mafia. There was a large fresh flower arrangement placed at the memorial. Zucchetto was also working with Commissioner Ninni Cassara, who was killed in 1985. Rita Zucchetto, Calogero's sister, started an organization called "Libera" to educate Italians about the Mafia. She also started "Addiopizzo," the organization that protests businesses paying protection money (pizzo) to the Mafia. Eventually, Rita was elected to the European Parliament.

The airport in Palermo has been named The Falcone-Borsellino Airport after the separate killings of Judge Falcone and then two months later Investigative Judge Borsellino by car bombings in 1992. In 2006, *TIME Magazine* named them among the top heroes of the last sixty years. In Palermo, there is a memorial at an intersection with a special tree planted for Borsellino. Every year in Washington, D.C. there is a mass and a service honoring Judge Falcone.

A quantum leap in Sicilian crime occurred in the late 1950s, when several cosche joined the rapidly expanding international drug business. A formal decision to that effect was taken when Sicilian and U.S. mafiosi held a meeting in the Grand Hotel et des Palmes in Palermo in October 1957. The local authorities were aware of the Mafia conclave but did nothing to break it up. The participants included a nephew of the late Don Calo, Giuseppe Genco Russo, whom many cosche then acknowledged as the "chief of all chiefs"; Lucky Luciano; the Sicilian-American gangsters Joe Bonanno and Frank Garofalo, and other criminals.

The Sicilians thought that the Sicilian-Americans had abandoned the feudal presences of their fathers. They no longer pretended to be interested, especially in peasant justice for the oppressed. They were interested in making money in drugs. That meeting was followed a few weeks later by the famous conference at Appalachia, New York, which was raided by state police and federal agents. Soon Sicily became an important link in the East-West narcotics traffic.

The Pizza Connection Trial started in 1985, my first year in Witness Security. That was my introduction to the wide range of characters from the top to the bottom of both the Sicilian Mafia and the American La Cosa Nostra. At the time Tommaso Buscetta was the most important defector from the Sicilian Mafia and the highest ranking to defect. In the world of international narcotics trafficking, Buscetta picked up where the French Connection left off. In the 1980s, he had been arrested in South America. Sometime later he began cooperating with the Italian and U.S. authorities. By this time, over a dozen of Buscetta's family had been killed in Sicily. He also testified at the other important maxi trial in Palermo, where 452 mafioso were on trial in the Ucciardone prison, and a special courtroom was built with cages that housed the hundreds of defendants.

When Buscetta testified in the Pizza Trial, he was not protected by Wit/Sec marshals from NY Metro. As far as I know Buscetta never wanted our Program because of the rules and regulations. Two DEA agents, Mario Sessa and Tony Petruci, took care of Buscetta. However, they would reach out to us if they needed something. The first time I met them all together, Buscetta would not look at me. He acted very proper. The next time we met the agents introduced me to him and we shook hands as a result of the introduction. After that when we met, he would smile and nod. When I looked at him, I could tell something was off. I guessed he had plastic surgery to alter his appearance. His face was somewhat puffy and a little distorted. In 2000, Buscetta passed away from cancer at age seventy-one in the United States.

Similarly, XXX followed the same script as Buscetta. Both men had been heavily involved with narcotics. XXX was a member of the Santa Marie di Gesu family led by Stefano Bontade, who was killed in one of the Mafia wars. XXX also testified at the Pizza and Maxi Trials. We produced him for the Pizza Trial in New York. He was kept in a safe house and he was not in custody at the time. Most of his family, just like Buscetta's, had also been killed in Sicily.

I spent many days and nights with him. He always had fire in his eyes. I could see storm clouds ahead for him! The last I heard, he voluntarily returned to Italy after the completion of all of his cases in the United States. Back in Italy, he was arrested again and then finally entered the Italian Wit/Sec Program, but that "fire" in him got the best of him and he was arrested yet again! Who knows, he could still be sitting in jail!

At the other end of the Sicilian Mafia cooperating chain was XXX. He was close to the top of the list of the most troubled protected witnesses I ever met. Of all the witnesses swimming in turbulent waters, he was struggling against the current. To look in his eyes, one could see the desperation. XXX was always sweating. He was a contract killer who had killed about a dozen people. He told me once he had to kill a chef of a particular restaurant. He walked in and asked a waitress, "Who is a da cook?" She pointed to one of the chefs with a white hat on. XXX went in the kitchen and shot and killed the wrong man!

XXX testified in the XXX case concerning murders and narcotics. He also testified before the XXX. After testifying in court and being relocated into the Program, he called XXX in NY. XXX had represented one of the defendants in the case whom XXX had testified against. First of all, that phone call would be grounds for termination from the Program. He wanted XXX to come and visit him in his new location. Of course, he needed money. That is not unusual for some witnesses who enter the Program. According to news reports, XXX gave him money for expenses. He told XXX that he wanted to recant his testimony. I have no idea what he was thinking. He had signed papers and his visitors returned to New York and notified officials at the XXX. A few days later the government conducted a grand jury investigation. He pled XXX. As a result, he could have been thrown out of the Program. He could also have been reinstated and relocated to a new area. Every case is different. I heard he passed away, but I do not know the details.

This was an unusual case of a relocated witness wanting to recant his testimony and it was covered in the press. However, it was not protocol for us in New York Metro to be brought up to date on the fate of every relocated witness who came through our doors over the years. That would be a full-time job in and of itself. However, there would be times when we heard about witnesses in Wit/Sec World and their status. Those sources were either the relocation inspector, the case manager, or even the witness calling. There were many times when relocated witnesses would call me about issues or problems they were dealing with. I would always advise them to talk with their inspector or the supervisor in their area and then if they weren't getting results to call their sponsoring U.S. attorney.

The Pizza case opened up a whole new long-lasting relationship with the Italian government that not many in the Program understood at the time. The United States and Italy agreed to establish a working group to deal with issues between our countries' law enforcement efforts against organized crime. Italy also wanted to start its own Witness Security Program. All levels of the Italian law enforcement community came here to study our system. We also sent personnel over there. And after long, hard work, a Mutual Legal Assistance Treaty was established between the two countries. Part of the agreement was that the U.S. would accept witnesses from Italy into our Program, and we would produce them for testimony.

Italian Investigative Magistrate Judge Maurizio Laudi visited the New York office, and I was assigned to assist him in his travels to understand our system. In September 1988, I brought the judge to the Southern District of New York U.S. Attorney's Office, the

Eastern District, and the U.S. courthouses in both districts. For social activities the judge wanted to visit the World Trade Center, Central Park, and Wall Street. The judge had made an appointment to visit Mr. Michael J. O'Neill, the former editor of the *NY Daily News*, so I took Judge Laudi up to the Larchmont Yacht Club, where we went out on Mr. O'Neill's boat for an afternoon lunch.

Judge Laudi told me he brought his wife with him to New York, and I invited them to my house for dinner. On the weekend, XXX, who was assigned to the Wit/Sec detail, brought the judge and his wife to my house. The judge and his wife enjoyed their evening, meeting Elaine and our girls, who were the same ages as their children. He told me over dinner that he and his family were under twenty-four-hour protection in Italy.

After the judge returned to Italy, we communicated yearly, exchanging Christmas cards and photos. A few years later I received a call from AUSA Pat Fitzgerald, who asked if I could come over to his office. I showed up and Judge Laudi was there with some other officials visiting the U.S. Attorney's Office. We hugged. We all had a photo taken with the then U.S. Attorney Mary Jo White. It was the last time I saw Judge Laudi. In 2009, he passed away from natural causes. I watched his funeral on YouTube. I sent my condolences to his wife, and we keep in touch by email.

Two Italian anti-Mafia agents, Maurizio Ortolan and Franco Fabiano, came to New York on official business. I booked them into the Vista Hotel at the World Trade Center, took them around New York, and enjoyed their company. We went to Ellis Island, the Statue of Liberty, and other New York sites. They were interested in buying blue jeans and work boots that they said were very expensive in Italy. I had them over to my house and cooked dinner for them. When I brought them into our office, they could not get over how, in the morning, workers would stop to buy coffee in a plastic cup that was then put into a paper bag and carried to the office to be drunk at their desks. In Italy, they would socialize at espresso bars and stand to eat, talk, read the paper, and then go to work. Fabiano indicated how it is important in Italy to eat and drink with others. We had a few good laughs about the differences in our cultures. I became friends with Maurizio, who has since retired. Whenever I traveled to Italy and he was available, I would visit with him. I have met his family and have eaten at his house. We continue to exchange Christmas cards and emails.

In the early 1980s, there was a vicious second Mafia war in Sicily that claimed over four hundred lives. The first, in the early 1960s, caused Buscetta to flee Sicily for first New York and then later Brazil, where he was eventually arrested and extradited to Italy. He cooperated with Judge Giovanni Falcone and testified both in the U.S. and Italy. Another major witness to cooperate with Judge Falcone was XXX, an important chemist who cut heroin for the Sicilians. Judge Falcone considered him to be reliable. When it became known XXX was cooperating, his mother, aunt, and one of his sisters were murdered. His brother had previously been murdered. Because of this, he was brought to the United States with some of his remaining family members. I traveled out of state to conduct an interview with his family and him for the Program. The FBI debriefed him and housed them in a safe house at that time.

At the interview were two assistant U.S. attorneys from the Southern District, Jim Comey and Fran Fragos. XXX was to testify in SDNY in a narcotics case against XXX. Present at the interview were XXX, XXX, XXX, and XXX, along with an official interpreter. XXX was a very serious and solemn person. His XXX, who could speak English well, explained some of the details of the Program that he did not understand. She was very mature for a XXX and conducted herself well in such a stressful situation. He was very

quiet. There were many issues to address with this family entering the Program. One example concerned XXX's pension from the
XXX. Later it became known in the interview that he had committed
numerous murders.

Eventually, I made an appointment with the Italian Consulate on
Park Avenue. Elizabeth Colleo, administrative assistant, was very
pleasant and put me in touch with Deputy Consul General Carlo
Cornacchia. He was able to assist me with all my requests from
the Italian government in reference to assisting XXX and XXX.
Mrs. Colleo would call me to make sure everything was going well.
In time, I received invitations to their Christmas parties and other
social events. When I received official invitations, I would think
back to my days working at the Plaza Hotel, especially when Major
Savino, the director of security, informed me that I could not attend
the social reception for the Dali Lama. Tickets had been mailed to
the Plaza for me by the Dali Lama's assistant, whom I had met years
earlier. However, the major wasn't impressed. I was working in a
different world and a different place then.

After he was settled in the Program, XXX requested that his
goods from XXX be shipped to the U.S. in his new area. After some
debate in Wit/Sec Headquarters, it was agreed that the Italians would
pay for and ship the goods to the U.S. One day I received a call from
Wit/Sec Headquarters with all the details about his goods arriving
in the NY Port. This was after the bombing and killing of Judge
Falcone and Borsalino. At the time XXX was still the chief inspector and told me Headquarters wanted me to set up a bomb sweep of
XXX. He asked me if I knew anyone at Customs and I told him I
did. I called Customs Agent Dave Ripa, who was an old high school
friend of the family. I explained the situation to Dave, and he said he
would be back in touch with me with the details.

That night I was still in the office working, and the chief called me from his home. He told me Bob Van Etten, the SAC of Customs, called him and wanted to know what the hell was going on about a bomb in XXX in the New York harbor! I told him to have Van Etten call me and I would explain everything to him. Van Etten called back within five minutes, and I explained we were being proactive and cautionary. He advised me that the last thing he wanted was for some bomb to be in the New York harbor. He agreed that Customs would work with us and told me that Dave Ripa would be back in touch with me. The next day I called Dave and we worked it out without an incident. Dave later became the SAC at Customs. Van Etten retired and became the Port Authority inspector general. Sadly, both Dave and Bob have since passed away.

In the fall of 1991, I received a phone call from XXX in USMS Headquarters telling me that there was a request from the Italian government for XXX to go back to Italy to testify. Headquarters told me to call XXX, deputy chief of the division, and get his okay for me to travel overseas. XXX agreed we could make the move. XXX and I would be taking XXX to Italy to hand him over to the Italians, who would protect him during his stay and produce him for court in Italy. This was part of the international agreement. However, we had an issue with his travel ID. I visited my new friends at the Italian Consulate in New York who gave me new travel documentation for XXX in a "fuggazi" name. XXX did not have to appear in person at the consulate. They never knew who the travel documents were for.

In mid-November I was to travel with XXX and XXX to Italy. I was just getting over jet lag after a good night's sleep at home. I had returned home that day from an official trip to Hawaii where I had to interview a family hiding out on their own, awaiting approval to enter the Program. But that is another story.

The next night we flew to Rome, where we were met by the Italian Polizia di Stato, who took us to their headquarters. Driving in the quiet motorcade with the Italian agents, I thought about the threat against XXX, especially since his family members had been killed because of his cooperation. Besides the Italian police, I kept thinking, did anyone not authorized know we were arriving in Rome at that time with one hot potato? I trusted the Italians we had been dealing with. Even though I had been around Italians all my life, this was still a different environment in a foreign country. Would I be able to profile someone and pick them out as a threat? If the Italian police came to New York on a protective detail, what would they observe as a threat? In our office we had a saying for the description of some mobsters: "What was he wearing?"

"He was wearing the uniform." That meant he was wearing a matching sweat suit with gold chains around his neck.

I never saw men wearing the uniform in Rome. But what I did see were plenty of Vespa motorbikes and scooters. Motoring along some narrow side street in the motorcade, I noticed a middle-aged woman wearing a fur coat and high heels, driving a motorbike. Now that was a threat!

At the Operations Center, we met Inspectore Gesidio Pera and Dr. Francesco Gratteri. The Italians took care of XXX. It was a relief not to have to assume security duties while he was in the country. They also advised us to surrender our weapons in a gun locker that we could retrieve upon our departure. That was the original plan and we were happy with the way we were treated and how things worked out.

The next day the other inspector and I went to the U.S. Embassy, where we met my friends from SDNY, Domenick (Mimmo) Buda, Department of Justice (DOJ), and Alfredo Principe (FBI). I was also introduced to FBI Agent Carmine Russo, who had a son in the FBI. Carmine was Sicilian and in the 1970s went out to Tucson to investigate Joe Bonanno. I told Carmine that I was stationed in Tucson in the military and was at the U of A in the early 1970s. I never asked him who threw the explosive device at Bonanno's house.

Mimmo was very helpful in our relationship with the Italians. He would forward documents and interpret legal issues. Mimmo got us tickets for an audience with Pope John Paul II. After the mass an announcement was made that if anyone had any religious articles, to hold them up and the Pope was going to bless them. I had a small cross and rosary beads I had bought for my mother and also took out my marshal badge and held them up as the Pope blessed them. I would think about that moment a few years later lying in a hospital...

Mimmo's sister Rachael had worked as an interpreter in Southern District of New York (SDNY). Her husband, Joe Cincotta, was an FBI agent with whom I had worked in New York. Alfredo was also an interpreter and was instrumental in making sure everything got done smoothly with the Italians. He always had information that came in handy. Richard Martin had been the senior counsel for the Department of Justice in Rome. He was a former assistant U.S. attorney in SDNY and one of the prosecutors in the Pizza case. I heard him speak fluent Italian once in SDNY and complimented him on his proficiency. He told me he was fluent and how helpful it was in the Pizza case because in the courtroom the defendants spoke to one another in Italian/Sicilian and they did not think that Martin could understand them.

After we finished with our business, XXX and I visited his aunt and uncle who lived in Rome. The next day we split up: He went to visit his relatives in Calabria, where his family came from. I took leave and traveled by train up to Trentino. The train stopped in the city of Trento, where I spent the night. The next morning I continued by bus over the mountains into the Val di Fiemme. I called and visited a family friend, Paola VanZetta, and she invited me to stay in her house in Ziano, another small town near Panchia in the valley. Her late husband, Tony, was a good friend of my father's. After Tony passed away, Paola moved back to Italy.

I took Paola to visit my relatives in Panchia. Aunt Elena, whom I had met with Elaine and my brother Larry back in 1978, had passed away a few years earlier. I had recently made contact with cousins. They had never met Paola. I spent time with my relatives, who took me around the valley, and we visited Cavalase, where my father's mother, Rosa Vanzo, was born. She lived upstairs from us when I was growing up and we referred to her as "Nana Up." She was one feisty woman! She used to throw buckets of water out the upstairs window at us when we were playing in the yard because we were too noisy. She was always yelling at us, but she made the best homemade peanut brittle as an afternoon treat. She was also renowned for her homemade grappa! She passed away in 1955 when I was eight years old.

The Val di Fiemme is recognized as "The Valley of Harmony" for its precious "resonance trees," which are used to create harmonic boards for pianos and violins, already appreciated by Stradivari and now by flute makers from any corner of the world.[6]

In 1998, an American U.S. Marine plane was flying low through this valley. The jet's wing clipped the cable of a cable car that extended across the valley. A cable car was in midair, traveling across the valley at the time. The cable car crashed to the ground, killing twenty Italian and German tourists and skiers. The cable car operator's last name was Vanzo, which was my grandmother's maiden name but no relation to us. The American pilot was supposed to stay above a thousand feet altitude during training flights. At a U.S. Military Court at Camp Lejeune, North Carolina, he was acquitted of involuntary homicide and manslaughter. The Italians were not happy with that decision.

In the meantime, while I was in Val di Fiemme, I called Elaine and told her I hadn't slept in three days because the Italians were filling me up with espresso! I am not a coffee drinker, let alone an espresso drinker! Finally, I returned to the States, but XXX stayed in Italy. I returned to Italy a month later. XXX finished his testimony so we brought him back to the States. However, this time the Italian Polizia di Stato assisted us in getting XXX safely out of the country. My friends Maurizo and Franco accompanied us back to the States. When we arrived in New York, I put them up in the Vista Hotel once again, where they were *contento*.

In 1999, an inspector from Headquarters and I traveled to Italy to interview one of XXX's family members who was an applicant for the Program. FBI Agent Rick Demberger also came with us. When we arrived in Rome, we were met by our friend Alfredo Principe, FBI. Alfredo escorted us through Customs without any delay. While in Italy, Alfredo told us he knew of a good tailor. He introduced us to his friend, and I picked out a fabric and had a Zegna suit made at a bargain price. I had to go back three times for proper fittings. While there I also met with Dominick Buda again. I got to visit with his wife and children, whom I had known. They had beautiful children, and we would exchange Christmas cards.

For some time now, I have been an admirer of the seventeenth-century Italian painter Caravaggio. Some of his masterpieces are located in little churches around Rome. I had asked XXX and Rich if they wanted to join me in locating some of the paintings. We were lucky because the churches were open and we got to see a few, which were very inspiring. I especially admired the masterpiece "The Calling of St. Matthew" in the San Luigi Dei Francesi Church. There are also other Caravaggios in that church. Believe it or not there was very little or no security around the paintings. Now that I think of it, there were very few people in the church that day.

XXX and I talked about how absorbing the paintings are. The paintings are in the side altars, perfect dramatic locations because the churches are not well lit. Caravaggio uses the technique of light and dark known as "chiaroscuro." However, his paintings are very vivid. Caravaggio's use of light and dark make me think of the mobsters who operate in their secret society in the shadows. Life is divided into light and darkness. If you are in one, you are not in the other.

XXX and I also visited again with his aunt and uncle in Rome. During our visit, his uncle looked at us and said, "Whenever you guys come over here, there is news in the Italian papers about changing governments and Mafia connections." We just laughed. We never said anything to him about XXX. Later, XXX would testify against a former politician who was indicted for Mafia association, which is against the law in Italy.

In 2000, arrangements were made for XXX to testify in Italian courts via secure video conference in the United States in a neutral location, instead of producing him in Italy. I traveled twice to different neutral sites in the U.S. to meet with him. We would go on video that had a secure connection to the courtroom in Italy. Without revealing my name I would identify myself as a marshal and verify his identity. He was usually wearing a disguise to alter his appearance. I exchanged Christmas gifts with him. That was the last time I saw him.

In October 2000, I received a phone call and fax from XXX in our headquarters in D.C., advising me of an Italian Parliamentary Commission traveling to D.C. and New York to study our system. They were members of the Italian Parliament, judges, prosecutors, and members of the Italian Anti-Mafia Commission. Headquarters asked if I could show them around SDNY. The following week I made appointments with personnel to explain the different parts of our system.

Upon the commission's arrival in New York, I showed them around the SDNY Federal courthouse. I introduced them to AUSA Joe Bianco, SDNY, who explained his role in the process of placing a threatened cooperating witness into the Program. FBI Supervisor Tom Uber and Special Agent Pat Luzzio provided information on their roles. The delegation also wanted to visit a correctional facility that housed Wit/Sec prisoners. I made arrangements for the following day and brought them to XXX and had them tour the XXX. Dottore Arturo DeFelice from the Ministero dell'Interno and a member of the Anti-Mafia Commission was very pleased with the arrangements and tours. He presented me with a medallion.

In 1997, I traveled to Palermo, Sicily, with AUSA Pat Fitzgerald, SDNY, to interview an applicant for the Program. Alfredo met us in Rome and traveled with us to Palermo. I do not know if the subject ever entered the Program. The Sicilian Anti-Mafia police were very professional and treated us well. I would say this trip was one of my most memorable. I am sure you will understand why after reading this chapter.

Upon our arrival, we were met at the airport in Palermo and driven to the Sicilian Anti-Mafia Police headquarters, which was surrounded by policemen armed with machine guns. We met with Antonio Manganelli, the *questore* for Palermo, and Santi Giuffre, his assistant. The questore is in charge of all law enforcement activities in Sicily. After conducting business, we went to a local restaurant for lunch, but Manganelli did not join us. I thought it was a little strange but learned later why.

We settled in our Hotel Politeama near the Politeama Opera House. Two Italian agents, Gabriella Giuntini and Salvatore Gentitle, met us at the hotel. I had asked Gabriella where I could buy my wife, Elaine, some jewelry. They took me to a jewelry store called Gioielleria DiPaola, where Gabriclla knew the owner, and I bought Elaine some gold jewelry. They took me around Palermo to historic sites and when I returned to the hotel, Alfredo advised me that we were invited to dinner that evening at the residence of Antonio Manganelli.

That evening, one of the Sicilian agents picked Pat, Alfredo, and me up at the hotel to go to dinner. We drove back to the police head-quarters. We thought the driver had to get something but he told us to follow him. We walked past the police guards with the machine guns, entered the building, and took an elevator that opened up into a private apartment. This was unexpected. Manganelli lived above their headquarters, protected twenty-four hours. It was then that I realized that this guy wasn't going to take a stroll with us to have lunch. It would have caused too much of a commotion. Upon my arrival in Palermo, my antenna went up when we checked into our hotel and when we traveled around with the Sicilian agents. But now visiting the questore in his private apartment, surrounded by guards, increased my fear factor. I was aware of the number of officials who had previously been killed in Sicily by the Mafia. That was unheard of in the United States.

But Manganelli lived well considering the circumstances. He wasn't hiding in some cave like some of the Mafia bosses on the run. The very large and spacious apartment had exquisite furnish-ings. Manganelli introduced us to his children and wife, who spoke perfect English. They also had a large golden retriever dog. Santi Giuffre was also there with his wife. We had a very enjoyable eve-ning. When I returned to my hotel room, sitting on the bed was a package. I didn't touch it. I called the front desk and asked who delivered the package to my room. The clerk said it was the woman who had picked me up earlier in the day. I opened it and there were two sets of gold earrings—gifts from Gabriella for my daughters,

Catherine and Theresa. Unbeknown to me, she bought them when we were at the jewelry store.

The next day we did more sightseeing. We drove past the location where Carabinieri General Della Chiesa and his wife were assassinated in 1982 while they were on their way home from his office. He had led the Italian government's offensive against political terrorism in the 1970s. Fifty-seven days after his appointment as anti-Mafia high commissioner, he was killed. There is a memorial there and still police are posted at a family member's residence. We drove past the des Palme Hotel, where that important meeting took place in the 1950s between the American and Sicilian Mafioso. They showed us Ucciardone prison, where 475 defendants were held in cages during the Maxi-trial that took place inside the prison. We walked around the famous Vuccria food market and I took some interesting photos. We visited Monreale with Gabriella and Gaspare Augugliaro, another agent who was very informative. We also visited the church of Santa Caterina in Piazza Bellini. It is very ornate and overwhelming. To say that about a church in Italy gives you a hint about the use of marble and color in this church… Oh, I forgot I was over here on official business!

With the assistance of the Polizia di Stato, arrangements were made for the interview of the subject to take place the following day. Alfredo was instrumental in acting as the interpreter and coordinating the arrangements. He consulted with Pat and me about the details he was hammering out with the Sicilians, who were very accommodating. The following day the interview was conducted and completed without any incidents.

That evening the agents took us to a restaurant outside of Palermo in the countryside called Crapa Licca. The agents were friends of the owner. The food was fantastic. The waiters wore traditional Sicilian outfits of high boots and vests. Since we had finished with our business, I told Pat I was going to make plans to visit my relatives in Sicily for a few days. I asked him what he was going to do. He said he, too, was going to visit his relatives. I said, "You have relatives in Sicily?"

His response was, "No, I am going to stop in Dublin on the way back to New York."

The Sicilians were very generous with presenting us with gifts. I presented them with USMS hats, pins, patches, and key rings. I felt embarrassed. They gave me two plaques, a hat "POLIZIA," an official beret with the Italian pin, and a large Sicilian marionette in armor with a sword. Marionettes are still considered part of Sicilian folk culture. Pat also received gifts, including a large traditional, colorful, painted Sicilian cart.

Gaspare asked me where my relatives lived and if I had their telephone number and address. I told him they lived in the Enna area out in the middle of Sicily. Because I am not fluent in Sicilian, Gaspare called and spoke to one of my relatives to make arrangements for a location to meet. Gabriella and Gaspare drove me all the way out to Calascibetta to a store in the village that was owned by my relatives, about ninety miles from Palermo. That was so generous and thoughtful on their part. I was expecting to either rent a car or take a bus and suggested that to them. They would not let me and did not want to hear about me doing that.

On the mountain opposite the city of Enna stands Calascibetta. The town, which benefits from the glorious mountain setting, has a natural amphitheater nestled in the rocky hollow on the side of a hill. The town was founded during the Arab occupation. Built by the Arabs, it was given the name Kalath-Scibeth, "the castle on the summit," named for the town's particular geographical position in order to fight and occupy Enna during the bloody wars between the Christians and Saracens. Fortified by Count Roger in his successful attempt to take Enna in 1087, it still retains a strongly Arabic and medieval feel in its narrowly twisting cobbled streets.[7]

When we arrived, we drove slowly into the town square (Piazza Umberto), where there were some elderly people standing around. Others were following the car on foot down the narrow street to the storefront. While we drove through the small square, there were some older men in long overcoats and hats, conversing. These men reminded me of my uncle Charlie, who stood less than five feet tall and always wore a long overcoat as well. Now I understood. It was their custom. Their eyes and turned heads, all the while, were following our car as we slowly passed by. Caspare said, "Those men know we are police even though we are in an unmarked car." We stopped in front of a grocery store. I met my Nanny's niece Cecilia and her family. I had a small overnight bag with me. Some young men wanted to carry my bag. Cecilia said it was okay. Gaspare gave me a cell phone and told me to call him in the next few days and they would come back to pick me up at any time. They told me, "There is nothing around here, you are out in the middle of nowhere, and there aren't even any hotels in the village." With a smile on their faces, they said they were going back to Palermo. Ciao! Ciao!

Cecilia was ecstatic that I was visiting. I had exchanged Christmas cards with her over the past few years. She was in her eighties. She was my grandmother's niece on my mother's side. Her son and his wife ran a small grocery store near the square. Cecilia walked me up a long, narrow, steep staircase behind the store. Everything was cobblestone, concrete, or brick. I thought the steps would never end. By the time we made it to the top, she was off doing something else. I was just about ready to collapse. She was effortlessly breathing while I was huffing and puffing. Now I understood why my mother was able to easily walk up and down Mountain Avenue. She had

had early training for mountain walking. And, did I mention that she wore high heels?!

Cecilia's house was above the street and the other buildings on the side of the mountain. Most of those were built into the mountainside. You could look across the valley and see the other town of Enna perched on the top of that mountain. In between the valley is the main autostrada highway that goes from Palermo to Catania.

Cecilia and her husband, Vincenzo, had a garden in the side yard and on the roof! There was a street located further above the house that you could walk up to by accessing another steep staircase. They kept their car up on that street above the house. I thought about the hills back in my hometown and how much steeper these were. After dinner and drinking wine, I met some other relatives and neighbors. My bedroom was very large with a separate bath. That first night I lay in bed under a crucifix above my head on the wall. I thought about my mother's mother, Marietta, who lived down the hill from us in New York and was known as "Nanny Down." She was soft-spoken, a great cook, musical, and very religious. Although Nanny Down could only speak Sicilian, we could understand her... sometimes. She was very stout and strong. On hot summer days, she would sit on a bench in front of her house that faced the street, saying her rosary and fanning herself. I remember walking past her house one warm day with a girl when I was in high school. She happily called us into the house to fix us a cool drink. She was overjoyed to see us and, of course, wanted to fix us something to eat. She was very devoted to her faith and the Blessed Virgin Mary. I am sure that when she emigrated she made sure she continued practicing her religious beliefs and passed them down to her children. I think that was one reason my mother was also very pious. I am sure they were all proud of Aunt Jo when she entered the religious life as a nun. Nanny Down passed away when I was in the military in 1967.

It was easy to doze off and I had a very good night's sleep. However, around daybreak, I was awakened by the sound of horse shoes clacking along on the cobblestone street below. I opened the shutters and looked down and could see a farmer on his horse bringing in fresh produce. I threw on some clothes, grabbed my camera, and quietly went down to the street. The farmer was very willing to have his picture taken. I was able to take photos of him and his decorated horse.

Later that day, Cecilia and Vincenzo drove me around the area. We visited the church (Chiesa Madre) where Nanny Down was baptized. They also drove me over to the next village, Villa Rosa, where my mother, her sisters Rosie and Josephine, her brother Coloergo, and their father were born. I took some photos. Cecilia wanted to stay in the car while I walked the streets with her husband. I asked him if he knew of any relatives on my grandfather's side who were still living in the area. He said there were none remaining. I wondered why that was. I walked past a political club; inside were elderly men playing cards. While out on the sidewalk, I took a photo through the open door and the occupants. They were not too happy! They asked Vincenzo who the guy was taking pictures. Vincenzo said to me, "Andiamo, andiamo."

After a few days I called Gaspare. He and Gabriela came out and picked me up. Before I departed I exchanged gifts with Cecilia and her husband. They gave me a scarf and hat. It was a most enjoyable experience meeting relatives and visiting the area. Without the assistance of Gabriela and Gaspare, it would have been much more difficult to make the journey that allowed me to visit my mother's early days.

I returned to my hotel in Palermo and stayed for a few more days of sightseeing before returning to Rome, where I met up with Maurizio Ortalan, my friend with the Polizia di Stato. I also got together with Mimmo and his family and Alfredo. I made my customary trek to the store in the basement of the U.S. Embassy to purchase some wine to take home. I also visited the wine store a few blocks away and loaded up on wine and olive oil. I bought some Brunello and Barolo. I still have some of the bottles, including a Biondi-Santi 1987 Brunello and a Borgogno 1983 Barolo. I think they may be ready to taste! I was carrying a lot of bags on this return trip, but I knew it would not be a problem getting through Customs. Upon my arrival at JFK Airport in New York, I was met by other USMS personnel who assisted me.

Of all the high-profile Sicilian cooperating witnesses who entered our Program, sadly it did not work out for some of them. XXX and XXX both left our Program after having major adjustment problems. They could not adjust to our culture, our way of life, and they did not have the epiphany needed to make a change.

I had spent many days and nights with XXX in different settings and locations both in Italy and the United States. He always thought that the Italian and American governments did not do enough for him. He realized that he needed to make a change. However, by his cooperation and the resulting deaths of his family members, the tradeoff was not worth it. I told him that some things you cannot put a price on. Many protected witnesses make choices to save themselves from prison and death. In the process they have to make difficult choices that sometimes do not work out for the better—for them or their family members. The rules and regulations for the Program are in writing. But there is nothing cut in stone for witnesses to follow when it comes to their personal choices concerning their future well-being.

There were other Sicilian witnesses who came into the Program, testified in trials in New York, and adjusted to the Program. Those Program participants were successfully assimilated into society in their respective relocation areas. They made the change. From 1985 to 1990 in SDNY, there was the Pizza Trial; the Commission Trial; the Castellano Trial; the Westies Trial; and the Gambino Trial, to name a few. Even in the District of New Jersey, there was one of the longest federal criminal trials in U.S. history going on against twenty-one defendants in the *U.S. v. XXX* trial. We produced many witnesses for that case. The U.S. attorney in New Jersey at that time was Sam Alito, the current Supreme Court justice. There were many more cases and trials going on during that time. Some of those minor cases would have been major cases in other judicial districts around the country. As word spread about the witnesses cooperating and entering our Program, more and more applicants were coming forward. A dynamic shift was about to occur between the districts.

It is difficult to assess the success of the Program in Italy. The official name of their Program is Servizio Centrale di Protezione, administered under the interior minister. It took the U.S. approximately forty years after our Program was created and laws were changed to reach the threshold of success. The Italian Wit/Sec Program is so much younger, and Italy is a totally different country with different customs and laws than the United States.

The *NY Times* published an article on July 7, 2013, "Taking a Bite Out of Crime," about a restaurant owner in Rome who refused to pay the "pizzo" protection fee to the Mafia. The owner went to the police after extortion threats. Four months after the extortion, the boss who ordered the threats was arrested and convicted. The restaurant owner has opened other restaurants since then. He buys his goods from anti-Mafia entrepreneurs who also are anti-pizzo. "Many come from Libera Terra, an anti-Mafia cooperative that farms land seized from the Mafia and, through community service camps, demonstrations, and events, works to raise awareness of organized crime worldwide."

An example of how things have changed in Sicily is the arrest in 2006 of Bernardo Provenzano, who was in hiding for forty-three years. Provezano was a Mafia boss from Corleone. He was convicted along with Salvatore Riina and others of the killings of Judge Giovanni Falcone and Paolo Borsellino. Provenzano died in an Italian prison hospital in 2016. His son Angelo gives talks to American tour groups in Sicily about his life growing up until he was sixteen years old, living on the run with his father. There are Sicilians who do not want tourism linked to the Mafia in order to make money.

Recently, Pope Francis called the Ndrangheta "an Adoration of evil and contempt of the common good. Those who in their lives follow this path of evil, as mafiosi do, are not in communion with God. They are excommunicated" (BBC June 21, 2014). Ndrangheta is another organized crime group in Southern Italy that is also involved in narcotics.

Antonio Manganelli, the former questora of Palermo whom I met in Palermo in 1997, went on to Rome to become the deputy police chief for Italian police under Gianni De Gennaro. In 2007, Manganelli became police chief of Italy. On March 20, 2013, he died in a Rome hospital after having surgery for a brain tumor.

7

1990–1993

"I'm not worried about Italians. They're just a bunch of opera singers."
                                        —Franklin D. Roosevelt

As a result of the additional cooperation between the U.S. and Italy and the increased number of Sicilian witnesses and cases, our workload in New York was ever expanding. The U.S. Attorney's Office in SDNY had its own criminal investigators. I was friendly with two of the investigators, Benny Serino and Jimmy Nauwens, who are both retired. There were many days when they would come to our office or I would go to theirs to discuss issues that may have developed between witnesses. They would relay any information to our office that was relevant to the Program. There was another office in the U.S. Attorney's Office on a different floor where Kenny McCabe shared space with Harry Brady. They were both former NYPD. Kenny was well known in law enforcement as an expert on organized crime. He always had his ear to the ground. He would call me to visit him in his office and give me an updated list that he produced of the membership of the five organized crime families in New York. We sat around and talked about the witnesses and prisoner witnesses in the Program and some of the issues that the witnesses would call Kenny about. I would relay the information to either the sponsoring assistant U.S. attorney or the case manager in our headquarters. Kenny would ask me for assistance in solving their problems. Some would call him from their relocation area. Some witnesses did not want to go to their marshal on certain issues. One witness who would call often was XXX. AUSA Dave Kelley, chief of the Organized Crime Section at the time, would also come in and join us in our discussions to come up with solutions. I was very deeply saddened when I heard Kenny passed away in 2006 from brain cancer. He was fifty-nine years old.

In January of 1990, the chief inspector told me that *60 Minutes* wanted to interview Program participant XXX. He was a member of the Westies, a violent crime group in Hell's Kitchen on Manhattan's West Side. XXX was involved in several murders and was in jail for one he did not commit when he cooperated. He became a protected prisoner witness. He had testified in the XXX case and other OC cases and had received plenty of news coverage about his life of crime.

The chief gave me paperwork from Headquarters to meet with a producer from *60 Minutes* at their offices on W. 57th Street. On January 4th, I met with Mr. Jeff Fager, and we went over an agreement where CBS would pay all of the expenses for the production of XXX and reimburse the government for expenses of USMS personnel. I also requested the names and background information on all the CBS personnel present for the interview. We signed a reimbursable agreement which also outlined the security details on the day of the interview. I met with Mr. Fager again on January 10th when we finalized the agreement, and I received the payment from CBS.

On January 13, Steve Kroft, a *60 Minutes* correspondent, interviewed XXX. During the interview, Kroft laid the groundwork of all the crimes and killings XXX was involved in and his life in the Westies. Kroft asked XXX a hypothetical question, and I para-phrase: "If, in your new relocation area, you are looking for a park-ing spot and someone happens to cut in front of you and takes your parking spot, what would you do?"

XXX kept his composure and said he wouldn't hurt anyone over that incident. XXX had a violent past and was feared on the street. He had been imprisoned for a murder charge. XXX cooperated with the DA to tape record other gang members for proof that XXX did not commit the murder for which he was presently imprisoned. XXX was released from XXX and went into federal custody. He had to undergo intense psychological testing in order to be cleared to enter the Program. While he was incarcerated in a XXX, SDNY, U.S. District Court Judge Sweet wanted numerous tests done on him before he released him.

Another marshal and I were taking XXX to a hearing before Judge Sweet concerning his release into the Program. He was dressed in a suit and loafers. While we were walking down a flight of stairs, he slipped and fell, but we caught him before he hurt himself. He said his wife had just bought him new Italian loafers. I looked at the shoes and told him, "An XXX has to be careful walking in Italian shoes!" Some Westies members were known to have some dealings with the Gambino crime family. There were a lot of people in law enforcement who were supportive of XXX and wanted him to be released from prison and enter the Program and succeed. I think he went through more psychological testing than the average applicant to get accepted into the Program. After XXX and his family entered the Program, we never heard about any major issues with them. They returned to New York a few times for official court proceed-ings and seemed to be very well adjusted. They have been a success story with their adjustment in Wit/Sec World.

My other experience with *60 Minutes* happened also in the

1990s, when they interviewed XXX. In his prime, XXX was a drug kingpin when he appeared on the cover of the *NY Times*. President Carter saw the article and ordered the government to go after him at any expense. He was arrested and convicted and sent to prison. Years later he cooperated and was brought back to New York, where he testified against his crew and many others. He ended up in XXX, not knowing if he would ever be released. *60 Minutes* got the okay to interview him, and our office made arrangements for the interview to take place at the U.S. Attorney's Office in SDNY. I was present and we had XXX in a separate room while the TV crew assembled in another office where the interview was to take place. Mike Wallace, the correspondent who was going to do the interview, said to me, "We are ready for XXX to be brought in."

I told him, "We are waiting for Howard to sit in during the interview."

Wallace exploded, "HOWARD! What the hell is he coming here for?"

"This is Howard Heiss's office. He is the chief of the Organized Crime Section and he is going to sit in on the interview."

Wallace said, "Oh, I thought you meant Howard Safir."

I thought it a little strange how Mike Wallace reacted when he heard the name Howard. Later I found out why. A TV show had done a segment on the Witness Protection Program and interviewed Howard Safir, who at the time was associate director of the USMS and in charge of the Program for the marshals. Safir was interviewed and stated no one had been killed in the Program when they followed the rules and regulations. However, film clips of Program participants who had been murdered but were not in the Program at the time of their demise had previously been aired on a TV show. As a result, Safir sued the network.

XXX was a high-profile prisoner witness. His wife was connected to his case and was also incarcerated along with the other
members of his crew. He told me he cooperated because his wife
was fooling around with his crew members after he was incarcerated and his crew didn't do the right thing. After he cooperated, the
Program took legal custody of his children and they were placed
in a XXX. He had court order visitation rights. We would make arrangements for the visit in the New York area. An inspector would
accompany XXX into New York. He was very involved with XXX.
Sometimes when they met, we would provide a XXX for him to
help them with XXX. Their XXX was his main interest at that time.
He wasn't sure if he would ever get out of prison even though he
had cooperated and had testified numerous times. He told me that
since the President got involved it had become political, and no politician wanted to be associated with releasing him at that time. U.S.
Attorney XXX was fighting for him to be released. Finally, in the
late XXX, he was released into the Program. He also became a successful member of Wit/Sec World.

The times—they were a changing! The SDNY had a large number of major organized crime cases in the late eighties. When the
nineties arrived, it was like a huge tidal wave had rushed across
the East River to Cadman Plaza, where the Eastern District of New
York in Brooklyn is located. There had been a change in the U.S.
Attorney's Offices in both districts. Giuliani left the "Sovereign"
District and entered the political arena. Otto Obermaier replaced
Giuliani. One day my chief inspector told me, "Come with me. We
are going to meet the new U.S. attorney with Louie."

AUSA Louie Freeh, Chief of the Organized Crime Section, at
that time, brought us into Obermaier's office and introduced us. The
chief inspector gave a brief update on the Program. Obermaier was
very quiet and didn't ask many questions but was a gentleman. The

meeting was quick. A few years later while he was still U.S. attorney, he was mugged leaving the office on his way down the subway stairs under the Municipal Building. He was not injured. He gave up a small amount of cash he had in his pocket.

A few years later Giuliani was elected mayor of NYC. One day at work my supervisor asked me if I wanted to go visit my old stomping grounds, the Plaza Hotel. He said there was a party for Rudy. After work we ventured out that evening. I showed my supervisor around some of the locations that were still operating like the Oak Bar and Oak Room. We then decided to head up to one of the ballrooms where the party was. We went to get into one of the elevators and at the same time in strolled Donald Trump with his security. We all introduced ourselves and said we were with the U.S. Marshals. Trump asked, "Who is that old marshal downtown that I always see on the news holding onto a celebrity coming down the courthouse steps?" We told him it was Romolo Imundi, aka "The Roman Gladiator." We all had a laugh. It was true. Once for the Columbus Day parade, I took some of my family and we were standing near St. Patrick's. When the parade approached, I looked up and there was Imundi walking along with and in a tight grip on the arm of the grand marshal, Sophia Loren! Imundi passed away a few years ago.

Attorney General Dick Thornburgh reorganized the U.S. Attorney's and got rid of the Organized Crime Strike Forces in the U.S. Attorney's Offices around the country. Around this time, John Gotti beat two indictments: one from the Manhattan DA, and the other from EDNY in Brooklyn. Did the government lose one of those cases because of the threat of reprisal in the jury pool?

Now, the third try was up for a good fight between all three jurisdictions to get another shot at Gotti. A nasty battle was fought and there was interagency infighting. After a sit-down at the Department of Justice in D.C., the EDNY was chosen to go after Gotti with a

RICO charge. After that decision Walter Mack, AUSA, SDNY, quietly resigned.

Mack had Castellano on trial in SDNY when Castellano was shot and killed in 1985. The highly publicized assassination in midtown Manhattan led to Gotti taking over the Gambino crime family. AUSA Mack had successfully prosecuted the Roy DeMeo crew of the Gambino family—violent killers who dismembered mob victims. We had a handful of witnesses in that case. A couple were XXX and XXX. They were both incarcerated at the same time. However, when one's time was up, he made a deal that XXX would stay in prison with him until he got out. XXX was a car thief in DeMeo's gang noted for stealing cars and shipping them overseas to Kuwait. They were released together and entered the Program but never took that big step to change their lives. They couldn't make it in the Program. In a botched armed robbery attempt in his relocation area, XXX went in to hold up a video store with a shotgun. He was shot and killed. Not long after that incident, his partner, XXX, got into a confrontation with another man who shot and killed him with a shotgun. Two other members of the DeMeo crew were XXX and XXX, who owned XXX. XXX was shot and killed by other members of the crew. XXX was devastated. He testified against the Gambinos and entered the Program. There are tremendous psychological pressures in this life. It is very difficult to talk to these individuals and get a true sense of their feelings. Some do not want to talk about their lives. When they are relocated, they have to agree to psychological testing and counseling. Unfortunately, this does not always help. Out of desperation, XXX committed suicide in his relocation area.

In September of 1990, XXX, a relocated witness, returned to New York to testify in a narcotics case. Assistant United States Attorney Peters was the prosecutor. He was concerned about XXX's state of mind because he was having difficulty adjusting to his new life in the Program. He had previously attempted suicide and had a history of emotional problems. I was working the night shift when he came back to New York to testify. The night before he was to go on the witness stand, he was a nervous wreck. I stayed up almost all night with him, watching movies. He couldn't sleep and was fearful of going on the stand in front of everyone in the courtroom. He was afraid of everyone looking at him. I kept giving him encouragement and tried to keep him from going over the edge. No matter what that Hells Angel thought at my first interview a few years ago, I was no psychiatrist!

I told XXX he had to remember his cooperation agreement and he had to be coherent and testify credibly and truthfully. Otherwise, I told him he would be getting himself wrapped up in a trick bag and in worse problems and end up in jail. Working with witnesses meant that sometimes you never learned the true backstories of some of the issues pertaining to the witnesses and their relationships with the defendants, prosecutors, agents, and family members. Most prosecutors but not all would relay information to us that was relevant to the witnesses' well-being.

The next evening when I returned to work, I found out XXX had successfully testified and was already on his way home. Because of his testimony, the jury convicted the defendant. I don't know what happened to him after he returned to his relocation area. His fear of testifying was an example of the strain and mental anguish that has made some witnesses very despondent.

Also in 1990, U.S. Attorney Andrew Maloney, EDNY, and AUSA John Gleason were chosen to prosecute John Gotti. In September, an acting boss of one of the major crime families had started cooperating. At the time, XXX was in the Metropolitan Correction Center (MCC), New York, with Gotti awaiting trial. He heard about the boss "taking a turn" and that November, he also decided to start cooperating. The walls of the local crime families were crumbling. EDNY was about to get some new trials.

Around this same time, XXX, a Gambino informant, had been wearing a wire, working for the NY State Organized Crime Task Force. He testified in the John Gotti Trial in EDNY. He came into the Program with his girlfriend. The first time I met him, he told me I looked familiar and he thought he knew me from somewhere. We had some small talk and a quick conversation. I read his case file and discovered he had dumped a victim of a mob hit in the woods on a mountain not far from where I lived. Sometime later I was with him one day and he asked if he could call me at home if he had any problems in the Program. I advised him to go through his marshal first, but I gave him my home number to use in an emergency. One night Elaine answered the phone and said it was for me. I asked her who it was and she said, "Some guy with a tough voice." It was XXX, who was having problems with his girlfriend. She had left the Program and returned to NY. She would also call me for advice. I informed her that she left the Program and was no longer entitled to any more of our services. Two of the task force members, Tony Prococino and Ed Wright, were part of the team that sponsored XXX, and I worked with them in helping him succeed in the Program. Tony informed me that XXX had a former girlfriend who lived in my town. That's when I put it together about XXX saying I looked familiar. He passed away in 2003. Tony also passed away a few years before that.

The famous "Windows" case of bid-rigging was ongoing in EDNY. The defendants were from four of the five crime families in New York. The government's main witness was XXX. I had interviewed him for the Program at the Vista Hotel at the World Trade Center. Present were the late AUSA Charlie Rose, AUSA

Greg O'Connell, and Agent Dick Rudolph, FBI. XXX entered the Program without his wife and children. His ex-wife remained in New York and would call me whenever his name appeared in the newspapers, to complain about how XXX left his sons and how hard her life was. She would tell me he had enough money but never sent her any. I told her if she was having any problems to call Dick Rudolph.

When XXX was needed for the Windows case, he was on the stand for weeks. He had a bad back and had the judge's permission to stand while testifying. He was not in custody, and I only brought him over to EDNY one or two times. His mother was allowed to bring in home-cooked food for him while the trial was in progress. Trays and trays of homemade Italian food would arrive in the evening in EDNY. The U.S. attorneys and agents feasted. However, when the jury came in with the verdict, they had agita. The jury didn't believe all of his testimony.

Sick with cancer in the late 1990s, he testified against "The Chin" Gigante via closed-circuit video. He passed away in 1997 in his relocation area. Gigante was convicted and died in prison in 2005.

The Colombo War, which lasted roughly from 1990 to 1993, was heating up, and cooperators were knocking our doors down to get into the Program. They were looking for deals like XXX and XXX got. XXX told me once that the Program added another option for wise guys. Before "in the life" you either died in jail or were killed on the streets. Now there was a new opportunity for a new life. The Program was reducing the fear factor.

During the Colombo War, the Persico and Arena factions were battling, and approximately fifteen cooperating witnesses came forward separately. I received a request from Wit/Sec Headquarters to interview a large family for the Program. I don't know their status today, so I will not mention their names. However, I traveled out of state to interview them at a beach resort. When I arrived, I met the agents and the family. Also present was NYPD Detective Tommy Dades, who was assigned to the FBI Organized Crime Task Force. I had presented most of the information about the Program to the family and told them we would take a break. While in the restroom, I heard crashing and thumping out in the living area. I opened the restroom door and saw Dades rolling around on the floor with one of the applicants for the Program. The other agents were trying to break it up. After they were separated, they went at it again, this time landing out on a balcony. It was broken up again. I told everyone, "Let's take lunch!" The other agents took Dades out for a car ride to get some food. Believe me, it would be an understatement to say that there can be intense moments and emotions at an interview. Sometimes an applicant does not like to hear about the rules and regulations of the Program. Agents and prosecutors like to keep their witnesses happy and paint a rosy picture of the Program, but they are not allowed to make any promises or misrepresentations to the witnesses. So when an applicant is interviewed by the marshal, they may not like hearing about the realities that come with the Program. Like any other part of the government, getting some things done in a relocation area takes time, and sometimes there are legal complications. There is a lot of downtime—waiting, not knowing if things will work out for the witness and the family. This incident stemmed from a misunderstanding. Tommy Dades didn't do or say anything wrong, but the applicants weren't ready to hear what sacrifices they would need to make to survive—separating themselves from their old selves and embracing the new.

The chief inspector notified me one day that I had an important preliminary interview to do: It was XXX, acting boss of the Luchese crime family. I had known who XXX was from talking to Kenny McCabe. At that time the news was reporting that he was cooperating. I called the case agent, Bob Marston, FBI, to work out a date and I informed him of everything I needed and who should be at the interview. A few days later I received a call from Branch Chief XXX, in Wit Sec Headquarters. XXX was a former inspector in NY Metro. He told me that the chief of the division and managers were looking at this upcoming important interview with XXX. They wanted to make sure that everything went well from the beginning of the process to the relocation of XXX and his family. The branch chief said he would be coming up to meet me to sit in on the interview and address any issues that needed approval from Headquarters.

On October 29, 1991, we drove up to a hotel in Stamford, Connecticut. The FBI was housing XXX in the area. Also present at the interview besides the witness and Agent Marston were the sponsoring assistant U.S. attorney, Tony Siano, and another FBI agent, Jim O'Connor. Siano had made arrangements for XXX to select a private attorney from a standard list to represent him in upcoming matters. XXX didn't have any pending criminal charges against him. He picked Jim DaVita. I knew Jim. He was a former AUSA from SDNY and had prosecuted Leona Helmsley. I thought this was one of the first times XXX met DaVita. XXX stated, "We are mostly all Italians here!" He questioned DaVita as to his background and found out that he was from the same area in Brooklyn where he had grown up. DaVita's father was a doctor in the area. Later he found out from his wife that DaVita's father delivered one of their children. He was comfortable and relaxed. Just a few weeks earlier there had been an assassination attempt on his life, and his main concern was the safety of his family.

He was a short man with a solid build. He was an old-school gangster, a walking encyclopedia of the New York underworld. He was similar in size to my maternal grandfather. I sat there at that interview listening to him and DaVita talk about their younger years and their families. It brought back memories of my own family growing up in an Italian household with our Sunday dinners at my grandfather's house.

The witness told me after the failed assassination on his life, he feared for the safety of his family, so he moved them temporarily to Hawaii for safety. He figured none of the New York wise guys would be able to get any guns on a plane to fly there. This case was different than the usual because at the time he was a free man, not charged in any ongoing organized crime criminal case investigation. The majority of applicants for the Program are involved in a case and are either incarcerated or out on bail. Then they make a deal with the government and sign a cooperation agreement. According to XXX, he decided to cooperate after the failed attempt on his life. He called the FBI and asked for Marston, with whom he had dealt on a previous case, years earlier. He eventually got Marston on the phone and arranged for the FBI to pick up his son and him for protection. He had taken that first big step on his own. The opportunity was there and he committed himself to change. For him that was a huge leap into a new beginning.

A few weeks after the interview, I met Siano and Marston in Hawaii. Also with me was the chief inspector of that area. I interviewed the family. The other son, XXX, and his wife were not applicants at this time because they both had issues that needed to be resolved before they could be interviewed and accepted into the Program. The FBI had them in a safe location. However, they both had a tough time making it through. Eventually, they were able to resolve their issues and were then relocated. Unfortunately, one of them started to have serious medical issues and passed away. I received a phone call in my office from Headquarters advising me of XXX's death. I reached out to XXX and XXX to express my condolences to the family. Normally, it is against Program guidelines for applicants with XXX to be relocated for security reasons because many in this situation can be compromised.

When protected witnesses testified in federal, state, or local courts, a marshal would be in close proximity. Depending on the layout of the courtroom, sometimes you were within arm's reach of the witness. As a result of that closeness and depending on the witness and the drama of cross examination, you could feel the intensity of the moment. Considering the background of some of the witnesses, it takes courage and strength to come forward and testify against one-time friends and sometime blood relatives. Making a plea deal with the government and signing a cooperation agreement meant the witness could not lie or the agreements would be voided. Some have lied, some have returned to jail, and some have had their agreements ripped up. Most cooperators have corroborating evidence to support their versions of events. However, some truths never come out.

It would come to pass that over the next few years, I would hear XXX's testimony and description of the attempt on his life at the Kimberly Hotel in midtown. He was attending a meeting with other Luchese and Bonnano members in one of the hotel suites. According to XXX, he sensed that the actions and the remarks being made by members of his crew were threatening and that they were going to kill him. He was able to flee the hotel. When he got down to the street, his driver was no longer there waiting for him, which reinforced his idea that they were going to kill him.

After XXX entered the Program, he would return numerous times to New York to testify in a number of high-profile cases. I produced him for many of those testimonies. I remember sitting near him numerous times during his testimony. As always he would set the stage with background information about his upbringing, his neighborhood, his military service, his family, and his introduction to organized crime and the crimes he committed. He was feisty. He enjoyed the challenge of the confrontation with defense attorneys. He had a very good memory. I was present when he testified and was cross-examined by the late defense attorney James LaRosa. It was a classic matchup between two well-heeled veterans in their respective careers. I could see LaRosa was getting to him. XXX's blood pressure was rising and his cheeks were red. LaRossa was also getting hot as they bantered back and forth about the facts. I looked at them and compared them to two fine aged bottles of Italian wine: Barolo vs. Brunello!

The judge called for a break. We walked back to the witness room, and XXX was pacing like a panther, cursing about the defendants wasting their money hiring defense attorneys. He was ready for battle. The judge's clerk knocked on the door to let us know the judge was ready to resume court. XXX was out the door before the clerk was finished talking. When he approached the witness stand, he was like Ali entering the ring. But he wasn't going to do a "rope a dope." He was touting the opponent in the middle of the ring, asking for his best shot. I wasn't around when XXX returned to New York to testify in the "Mob Cops" trial in 2006 in EDNY, Brooklyn. I would have paid for a reserved seat to watch another classic matchup, this time XXX vs. Bruce Cutler.

Sometimes when XXX would come back to New York, he would ask me if he could go for a walk. In the cover of darkness, I would make arrangements for his security so he could walk, stretch his legs, and inhale some good NYC air that he missed so much. He liked to walk at night after dinner. Sometimes I would walk with him and he would tell me how he was surprised but impressed with the number of Italian-Americans in good federal law enforcement positions. He told me, "You should be out in Italian neighborhoods letting these young kids know what is available for them and to get them involved instead of them looking up to the wise guys." He also told me that he knew of NYPD cops who were Italian, but he wouldn't trust them. "No matter what organization you belong to, once you are labeled a rat, no matter if it is true or not, you are finished." I doubt in my lifetime there will ever be another witness like XXX.

In March 1991, the Wit/Sec supervisor in the Boston office and I took a relocated witness to Luxemburg. The witness, a member of a drug cartel, was involved in laundering money for the cartel. He was needed to testify in a trial in Luxemburg City. We flew into Brussels, Belgium, where we were met by Luxemburg federal agents who drove us into Luxemburg City. The witness, who was not in custody, testified for a few days. While we were in Luxemburg, the agents took us to a World War II cemetery where there were rolling hills with white crosses on the soldiers' graves for as far as the eye could see. The agents asked us if we could pick out the grave of an American general who was buried there. We walked around and looked but could not find the grave. They told us to turn around. Up on a small hill overlooking the graveyard was the grave of General George Patton. That was a very somber moment. The agents were proud of the fact that the people there appreciated the sacrifices of the American troops during World War II.

A few weeks after I returned from this trip, NY Metro assisted German agents from the Bundeskriminalamt, the German federal police responsible for international organized crime and federal witnesses. We welcomed them into our office and assisted them with the movement of a witness. As is customary, we exchanged agency memorabilia.

Michael Milken, the high-profile Wall Street financier, was indicted for securities fraud. This was the stock fraud of the century. Milken pleaded guilty and was sentenced in SDNY to ten years and a six-hundred-million-dollar fine. AUSA's Nelson Cunningham and Karen Patton prosecuted Milken for masterminding the fraud. He agreed to assist the government. The U.S. Attorney's Office requested Wit/Sec handle Milken during his cooperation. This was an example of our relationship with the U.S. Attorney's Office and the reputation of New York Metro. During the first week of June 1992, Milken testified in SDNY. His sentence was reduced to two years. He was housed for several days in seclusion from the press and the public. However, his wife and son were able to visit him. He was safely and discreetly transported to FCI Pleasanton, California, by XXX and myself.

During the time I spent with Milken, we had conversations on a variety of topics. He asked me if my wife worked and I told him she was a schoolteacher. He advised me of his interest in education reform in the United States. He showed me how he enjoyed solving math problems. Just a few years prior to Milken's arrest, Ivan Boesky was also arrested and sentenced to three years' prison time for insider trading. Boesky paid a hundred-million-dollar fine and also cooperated with the U.S. Attorney's Office in SDNY. We also handled Boesky. XXX and I transported him to the federal penitentiary in Lompac, California. At the time we moved Boesky, he had changed his appearance. He had grown a full white beard and had long white hair. The role of Gordon Gekko in the movie *Wall Street* was based very closely on Boesky, who was also on the cover of *TIME Magazine*. This was the time period of Wall Street excesses, with the slogan "Greed is good." What a difference in New York from the 1970s to the 1990s!

One day the chief inspector called me into his office. He told me he had a scheduling problem and asked if I would go to the Drug Enforcement Office the next day to give a presentation on the Program to a class of agents. I told him I would and he gave me all the contact information. The next day I showed up at the DEA's office and there were about ten agents present. During my presentation I noticed one person sitting right in front of me in the first row. He looked familiar and every time I glanced at him I tried to remember how I knew him. After my presentation there was a question-and-answer session and then it concluded. Everyone was getting ready to leave and the guy in the front row stood up. I said to him, "Are you from Cornwall?"

He said, "Yes."

I said, "Your name is Angelo Navarro."

"How do you know me?"

I told him I played basketball against him in high school and we used to beat them all the time! He couldn't believe that I remembered him. He told me he didn't remember me but remembered my friend John. I even told him he had older brothers who my older brothers played against. He was a NY State trooper assigned to the DEA drug task force. It just goes to show you, no matter what size school, town, or city you are from, you never know when you will meet someone from your past. Good or bad! And that is also on the minds of Program participants when they are living in a new area.

8

Arizona 1993

In early January 1993, I was out in Arizona on business. I was driving by myself and heading toward an intersection. That's the last thing I remember.

I awoke in what I thought was a dream. I was lying naked on a cold metal slab. I could hear people's voices. Without opening my eyes I felt my right hip for my gun but only felt my cold bare skin. I could still hear people talking. I opened my eyes and saw doctors and nurses hovering over me. There were bright lights shining down in my eyes. The doctors were asking, "Do you know your name? Do you know where you are? Do you know what day it is?"

I closed my eyes without saying a word, wondering where I was and what was happening. The next time I opened my eyes, I realized I was in a neck brace and the doctors and nurses were still all around me treating cuts to my forehead and the rest of my body. I was hurting all over. The doctors again asked me the same questions and I did not answer. I drifted off again. I don't know how much time elapsed, but the next time I awoke, I was still naked. There was a sheet covering me. This time there was a police officer looking down at me who said, "Who the hell are you? I have a nine-millimeter gun and a New York license with your photo in one name and another New York license with your photo in another name." He held them both up in each hand to show me.

I didn't say a word and closed my eyes again and went back to sleep. I was groggy. The next time I opened my eyes, the police officer was still there, but there was another man with him who introduced himself as security for the hospital, and said he was a retired deputy U.S. marshal. His name was Cliff Cline. He was holding my U.S. Marshal credentials and asked, "What are you doing here?" I tried to speak and he got closer to me. I managed to get out two words. He looked at me and then at the police officer and then he said, "Oh damn! Okay, now I know. Don't worry, we have your gun, your undercover ID and credentials. I will take care of everything."

The two words were XXX XXX, the senior inspector in the Phoenix Wit/Sec office. I knew him and had worked with him over the years. I closed my eyes and thoughts drifted away to another time and place when I had held up those credentials and badge to be blessed by Pope John Paul II in Rome just a few years earlier.

Hours passed. Still no one told me what had happened and I wasn't in any condition to ask. I could hardly put together what was going on around me. I went back to sleep. I could feel myself being moved and opened my eyes. I was being rolled on a gurney to have a CAT scan. I had a sheet and blanket over me. When we arrived at an elevator to go to the floor for the scan, we had to wait for the elevator to arrive. I was just getting my senses back. There were two attendants moving me. When they rolled me into the elevator, it was a tight fit and one of the attendants was standing near the elevator door when the door closed. I heard a horrific scream and the gurney started shaking. The attendant was yelling that his pant leg was stuck in the gurney wheel and the elevator had closed on his foot, twisting his ankle. The elevator doors opened and they pushed me out and I rolled down the hallway, coasting to a stop. The injured attendant was screaming and rolling on the floor. All kinds of bells and intercom emergencies were going off over the loudspeakers. I was just lying there in disbelief. I don't know how much time went by, but eventually another attendant came and got me. He told me the other attendant had a broken ankle. They eventually got me to the CAT scan and then sent me to a room.

The next day I awoke in pain and was hurting all over and I couldn't move. The nurses told me a doctor would see me later. The nurses showed me my clothes. They were cut up and looked like a pile of rags. When I was brought in the emergency room, the doctors and nurses had cut my clothes and underclothes off me. Now I was known as the patient who the attendant broke his ankle moving! Later a doctor showed up and told me I had been in an auto accident and asked me some questions, but I couldn't recall anything. He told me I had a broken neck, fracture of C5 vertebra, and a concussion along with cuts and bruises. As a result, the doctor told me I probably would never remember the accident. He was right.

That day didn't proceed much better. The chief of security at the hospital notified the supervisor in Arizona, who called the chief inspector in New York, who called my supervisor, who was also out in Arizona on assignment. At various times during the day, different personnel called the hospital and were told I wasn't a patient. Finally, the chief inspector called and wanted to know what the hell was going on out there and where in hell was Dapra. Cliff Cline had registered me under a *fugazzi* name, so the hospital staff didn't know Dapra was a patient!

Later that morning my supervisor showed up at the hospital with Cline, the chief of hospital security. They said the police department was still doing an accident investigation and wouldn't know what happened for another day or so because they were looking for witnesses.

Later that day Tom Morrissey, chief deputy of the District of Arizona, came to visit me with a female assistant U.S. attorney. Tom was a former deputy in Eastern District in Brooklyn. He was a friend and former coworker with my supervisor. That was the first time I met Tom. They also asked me questions I did not know the answers to. I thought the vehicle had blown up. I had no idea what happened.

That same day, the chief inspector called Elaine to inform her I had been in an accident and was in the hospital. Later I spoke to Elaine and told her not to worry, I was okay. I stayed in the hospital for an additional two days. The doctors told me I couldn't travel back to New York until I saw them again in a week. When I was discharged from the hospital, I told the nurses to throw my clothes away. My supervisor brought me clothes from my hotel room, where he would take me to recuperate. He was told to stay out there with me until I was able to return to New York. I stayed in bed for a week.

Cline and a police officer called and advised me that they found two different witnesses to the accident. One witness saw the subject vehicle speeding past the other witness and proceeded through a red light at high speed without braking or stopping. The subject vehicle continued speeding while approaching the next intersection. I was driving through the green light when the subject vehicle went through the red light and broadsided the vehicle I was driving. There was another witness driving behind the subject vehicle who stated the subject vehicle never applied his brakes. The detective stated that the driver of the subject vehicle was drunk and had AIDS. They suspected that he was trying to kill himself. The police officer stated that he didn't know if the subject was going to live.

My supervisor took me to the doctor's office for the follow-up examination a week later, and the doctor gave me the okay to fly back to New York.

At the Phoenix airport, the senior inspector of the Wit/Sec Office came out to assist us with pre-boarding. When he saw me, he shook his head and started laughing. He told the flight attendant, "You think he looks bad? You should see the other guy!" I knew him for a number of years. We worked details together and golfed together. He also thanked me for coming out to Arizona and wrecking one of his vehicles!

When we arrived at the New York airport, there were a couple of marshals to meet us. XXX drove me to my residence. I can still see Elaine and the girls' faces when they came out in the driveway to meet me. Although it was joyous to see them, it wasn't a pleasant moment for them to see me battered up and in a neck brace. They were about to get used to me being home for a while. It was better than the alternative.

I talked to the chief inspector and completed paperwork for worker's compensation until I could figure out what my options were. The doctors in Arizona gave me a list of doctors at Columbia University Hospital to follow up with my recovery. I chose a doctor who was also affiliated with Helen Hayes Rehab Hospital. I started outpatient treatments that lasted for months. Elaine and I talked about my options. I was about five years away from my first eligibility for retirement but didn't know if I could physically get back into a law enforcement position again. After about a year, I told Elaine I was ready to go back to my old job, and she supported my decision.

Around the same time, I received a call from XXX, deputy chief of the Wit/Sec division. He informed me that USMS legal counsel said I was no longer able to perform my position, so they were going to drop me off the rolls. I informed him that it was my intention to come back to work and that my doctors said I was going to be released from their care soon. He told me he would be back in touch with me. I told Elaine I was going to have to start working out to pass a physical and firearm qualifications. When my doctor gave me the okay to return to work, I started on an exercise routine.

At around the same time, I received a call at home from Frank Martin, younger brother of U.S. District Court Judge John Martin, who was the former U.S. attorney for the SDNY. I had last seen Frank at Judge Martin's swearing-in ceremony in New York. He informed me that he had just been appointed as deputy director of the Marshals Service at Headquarters and heard I was on compensation as a result of an auto accident. He told me if I was having any problems with anything to call him. I informed Frank that I was looking forward to going back to work. Unbeknownst to me, a few weeks later Frank happened to be talking to XXX, chief of Wit/Sec. Frank told XXX that he was talking to me and that I was coming back to work. A few days later I received a call from XXX, a case manager in Wit/Sec Headquarters. A few years later he became chief of the division. He and I had worked in NY Metro together years earlier. When he called, Elaine answered the phone because I was up on our roof fixing a leak. He was surprised to hear I was up on the roof. After we exchanged greetings, he asked me, "How do you know Frank Martin?"

I started laughing. I said, "You used to work here. You know his brother, the former U.S. attorney, is now a federal judge in Southern District. Why are you asking?"

He said, "Just wondering."

"Oh, okay." I never told him that Frank and I were former classmates. I knew someone had asked him to call me to find out what the connection was. I knew then that I was going to have to jump through some hoops to get back on the job, but it wasn't the time yet to "go to the well" and call Frank. I never ended up having to call Frank for any assistance. Unfortunately, he passed away not long after. I went and visited Judge Martin in his chambers to express my condolences.

Around this same time, I read in the papers that Milken had been released from prison. The article also mentioned that he was suffering from prostate cancer. He started the Prostate Cancer Foundation. I mailed him a get-well card through his attorney with whom I had dealings a few years earlier. Milken sent me a card of well wishes and for my own quick recovery from the accident.

As the days and weeks went by, I never heard from anyone in Wit/Sec. I was getting back in shape with no complications. I had a limited range of motion in my neck, but it wasn't debilitating and it was getting better. A few months later, I received a call from the chief of the division's secretary that a meeting was scheduled the following week in Washington between the chief and me. She asked if I could make it and I told her I would be there. I then called Larry Berger, chief counsel for the Federal Law Enforcement Officers Association, whose office was out on Long Island. I informed him of the situation. He told me he would go to the meeting with me.

Larry and I flew down to Washington and went to USMS Headquarters. When we arrived, the secretary wasn't there but someone else was filling in. I told her I had an appointment with the chief. She informed me that he was out of town and all his appointments were canceled. I informed her no one ever notified me of the cancellation. Larry and I were not happy and flew back to New York. A few weeks went by and I received another call from the secretary apologizing for the mix-up but that a new appointment was the following week. I called Larry's office, and he was out of town. His assistant Luciano informed me that he would go with me.

Luciano and I flew down and met the chief. He also apologized for the last mix-up with his schedule. The meeting lasted five minutes at the most. Basically, he asked me how I felt and when I wanted to come back. I told him as soon as possible. He told me he would call New York and work it out with personnel. We shook hands and he welcomed me back. Luciano never had to say a word, but I was glad for his support.

A few more months went by and I finally got a reporting date to go back to work. On my first day back after a couple of years away, I walked into the office at around 9 AM and it was quiet. No one was around. Inspector XXX was running operations. She was apologetic but said, "George, welcome back! I know this is your first day back, but everyone is busy. There is no one here. I need you to go to…" Blah, blah, blah… I was back in the saddle and happy to be there! The next week, I passed my FIT test and firearm qualifications. All was well.

However, a lot had changed in the office and Wit/Sec World. The former chief inspector had retired, my former supervisor transferred to the FBI Joint Terrorism Task Force, XXX, ex-New York inspector, left Wit/Sec Headquarters to come back to NY Metro as chief inspector. There was also a new inspector in the office. XXX came over from the District of New Jersey. After a few years he transferred out of NY Metro to Wit/Sec Headquarters. He was appointed by President Obama to be the U.S. marshal for the XXX. He invited me to his swearing in. Unfortunately, I couldn't make it.

Also, while I was out on compensation, the first World Trade Center bombing had occurred and that trial was completed. The Colombo Wars were over but some trials remained. XXX still had a few trials left to testify in. The volume of work had slowed down and so had the number of organized crime cases.

9

Elian

On November 11, 1999, Elian Gonzalez, seven years old, and his natural mother fled Cuba for the United States on a makeshift raft with eleven other Cubans. The raft capsized off the coast of Florida and all but Elian and another perished. Fishermen rescued them and turned them over to the U.S. Coast Guard. A long court battle ensued as to the custody of Elian and whether he should stay in the U.S. or be sent back to Cuba. Elian's natural father, Juan Miguel, traveled to Florida to take custody of Elian and bring him back to Cuba. Relatives in Miami fought in court to keep Elian with them. They refused to turn Elian over after they lost court battles to get custody. Attorney General Janet Reno authorized immigration agents to seize Elian. In April 2000, INS agents raided the Miami house and took custody of Elian. They then moved him to the Washington, D.C. area. The marshals were assigned to provide a protective detail on Elian and his father and family. News reports had Elian living at the Aspen Institute on the Wye River on the eastern shore of Maryland, which was not true but close enough.

The Wit/Sec Division was in charge of the detail. The assignment was a two-week, twenty-four-hour, seven-day rotating shift for the protective detail. A coworker from NY Metro and I drove down together at the end of April for our two-week tour. We attended a briefing on the operation. There were numerous fixed posts. There was always a Spanish-speaking marshal in close proximity to Elian. However, we gave him and his family room to live as close to a normal life as possible under the circumstances. That included using a swing and play set in the yard of the cottage they resided in. There was also a swimming pool nearby. Elian and his family were housed on a private estate/farm on the eastern shore of Maryland on the Wye River. The owner and occupier of the large property was Nina Houghton, an heir to the Houghton Mifflin publishing company. She was also a big contributor to the Democratic Party and President Clinton's campaigns.

The estate was surrounded by other large farms. Ms. Houghton, who was single, had local famers tend her land. From the main entrance you could not see any buildings on the property. All the major news organizations had full camera crews and reporters camped outside the main gate on a lone country road. Some of the local farmers were contracting for large amounts of money from the networks to park their trucks and equipment on their property and use their restrooms. There were no retail establishments for miles. We had personnel posted on the main entrance to screen official visitors. Bill Hufnagel, chief of the USMS Electronic Surveillance Unit, was there to oversee the installation of sensors around the property where our Special Operations Group was deployed. At the rear of the property there was a dock on the Wye River. A Coast Guard boat made periodic patrols of the waters.

After my coworker and I arrived, there was talk that Elian's classmates from Cuba were going to be authorized to come to the estate and stay with Elian. They all were going to go to class on the estate. One of the small outbuildings was converted into a classroom. The Justice Department and the State Department authorized the Cuban children, teachers, and doctors to come to the estate. I remember one typical "Friday night massacre."

In the government sometimes important changes, promotions, or new directives are sent out electronically late on Fridays for a number of reasons. In this case, after the Cuban students, teachers, and doctors arrived at the estate, the FBI discovered that one of the "pediatricians" was in fact a Cuban agent. The FBI wanted her deported and sent back to Cuba. The decision went to Secretary of State Madeleine Albright, who made the decision that the "pediatrician" could stay for the weekend and go back on Monday.

The classroom was off limits to all security personnel. The windows of the small building were covered so no one could see in. We would escort Elian and the handful of classmates to the classroom in the mornings. One day after the classroom was vacated, I peeked in one of the windows. I could see on the chalkboard a photo of Jose Marti, the Cuban revolutionary. There were writings in Spanish on the board. I think this may have been the first time that under the protection of the United States government—using U.S. taxpayer money, providing government security on private property in the United States—a non-U.S. citizen who also happened to be a minor from a Communist country was attending school here and being instructed by Communist teachers from Cuba.

On May 6, 2000, we had instructions to move Elian and his family to Washington, D.C. Juan Miguel and his family were represented in another court battle by Washington Attorney Greg Craig. Craig had represented President Clinton on his impeachment hearings and was at one time President Obama's White House counsel. Craig had a child around Elian's age. We were to bring the family to Craig's house for a private swimming pool party and then to Georgetown for a private dinner party later that evening. I was selected as shift leader, and XXX, chief inspector from Ohio, was the agent in charge. We knew as soon as our motorcade departed the estate, the news crew would follow. We had a Maryland State Police lead car escort us to the D.C. border, where we had a marshal riding in a U.S. Park Police car lead us into D.C. to communicate with the motorcade. We also made arrangements to have a lane shut down at a major D.C. intersection to lose the news crew.

As expected, as soon as we were spotted heading toward the gate to depart, the news crews started running to their cars and trucks to follow us. We were going with lights and sirens, and they were right behind us. In D.C., when we approached the blocked intersection, there was a long line of stopped cars. The lane that was shut down was the lane in the oncoming traffic in the opposite direction. The police had a few cones keeping that lane open. After we went around the traffic and used the blocked lane, the police blocked any traffic, including the news crews, from following us. We were then able to shut down the lights and sirens and proceed to Craig's house without the news crews knowing where we went. We spent that afternoon at Craig's house for the pool party. While there Craig mentioned to me a recent news item. The adjoining woods near his house were not far from the park where the jogger Chandra Levy was reported missing, and the police were still searching for her. Eventually, she was found murdered in the area.

After the pool party ended at the Craigs' residence, we headed into Georgetown. We arrived at the mansion of Mr. and Mrs. Smith Bagley on 29th St. NW. The residence took up just about a whole block. We had our motorcade parked along the side of the residence. XXX, my co-worker from New York Metro, who was one of the drivers, stayed outside with the vehicles along with some other detail personnel. Mr. Bagley introduced himself to me and gave me a little history about the residence. At one time there had been two adjoining townhouses. He purchased them both and had them combined with a central courtyard atrium, where the dinner was to take place. He hired a French architect to redesign the new house. The residence looked right out of *Architectural Digest* magazine. While holding a glass of scotch in one hand, he explained to me that the outside composition of the building was a light pink limestone. He then said, "Some people refer to this place as the pinko house!"

My response to him was "Better dead than red!"

He raised his glass to me and said, "Good one!"

He then took me downstairs, where there were photos of celebrities and politicians who had visited, including President Clinton with Mrs. Bagley. President Clinton had appointed Mrs. Elizabeth Bagley as ambassador to Portugal. At the bottom of the stairs was a grotto with an indoor swimming pool. Bagley told me President Clinton would come over occasionally for a swim. Later, the Park Police officers outside confirmed Secret Service details had spent a few times at the residence. I was also advised that when the Secret Service went there, they were OTR—"off the record." Mr. Bagley was an heir to the R.J. Reynolds tobacco fortune.

At the front door we had a guest list of people who had previously been screened. A marshal was posted there along with one of the Bagleys' household staff, Ellen Murphy, an elderly Irish woman. Among the guests were Greg Craig, his wife and son, along with their friends. Mostly all the American adults had ties to the ARCA Foundation, a pro-Cuban group.

After dinner it was painful to sit and listen to different attendees get up and talk about how great a country Cuba is and how better their way of life is. Later in the evening, my coworker from New York called me on the radio to say a news reporter was walking up to the front door. I advised the marshal at the door to step to the side and not answer the door. The doorbell rang twice. I got Ellen Murphy and told her, "There is a newsman at the door. Answer the door but don't answer any questions and don't tell him who is here. Try to keep it short."

The doorbell rang again and she opened the door. The newsman started introducing himself, saying, "Hi, I am from ABC News…"

Before he could even finish his introduction, Ellen said in a very heavy Irish brogue, "Go foock yourself!" and shut the door.

The other marshal and I were standing to the side. She looked at us and winked as she walked away. She was brilliant as the Irish would say!

I called my New York coworker and asked what was going on out there. He said that a news messenger was riding his bike down the street past the mansion and saw the parked motorcade and called the station. Within a half hour, the outside of the mansion was filled with cameramen and lights. We coordinated our departure by sending the Cuban relatives out the back alleyway while we went out the front door with Elian and his family. The newsmen got the photos they wanted. Then they followed us back to the estate. The Washington newspapers had some photos of us leaving. *The Washington Times* May 9th edition headline was "Elian gets a look at Georgetown Fat Cats."

Sometimes but not always after security details are completed, there is a common expression of appreciation by the principal, who presents a token gift to each member of the security detail. During the UNGA detail, some foreign ministers from certain countries were known as very generous with their gifts (watches, wine, etc.). There is a dollar value limit on the amount of the gift that the agent can keep according to government regulations. That range was between $250 and $500. However, not all protective details can be compared to the UNGA detail.

During the Elian detail at the mansion, Elian and his friends would play on a swing set or swim in a pool. We would sit around and watch them. It was a very relaxed atmosphere. One evening Juan Miguel was barbecuing dinner for his family. The Cuban head of Special Interests Section walked up to me and we had a brief conversation about the weather. Afterward he asked me if I'd ever smoked a Cuban cigar. I told him I had. A few days later I was at the front gate of the estate in the morning when a black Lincoln Town Car pulled up to the checkpoint. The news crews all started filming. The car was checked out and in the backseat sat the Cuban official. The window went down and he called to me. I walked over to the car and he tried to hand me a box of Cuban cigars.

I said, "No way!"

He started laughing and drove away. That evening I told XXX the story and how I thought he was trying to set me up. "Can you imagine CNN showing me accepting a box of Cuban cigars out of the back of the Cuban's official black Town Car!"

During our last week on the detail, Inspector XXX from NY Metro also came down to work the detail. He became the new lunch man. He would drive around the estate either on a bike or a golf cart with a little bell he would ring when he approached each manned post to take lunch orders. He would then drive one of our regular vehicles off the estate to a deli a few miles away. The first day he got lost! Everyone was complaining how long he took. I told him he was giving New York a bad name!

On the last day that XXX and I worked the detail, Juan Miguel called us to come over to the cottage where he was staying on the estate. He thanked us. He gave me an autographed photo of Elian and him that reads, "Cara George, Amore Recuerdo, Juan Miguel." He also gave me other personal photos taken in Cuba of him with Elian and his late mother and other relatives. He wanted me to know they had a normal family. I shook his hand and Elian's and wished them well. As I was leaving Juan gave me the box of Cuban cigars. We both laughed. From him, I would accept it!

In June, the courts ruled against the Miami relatives and in favor of Juan Miguel. Shortly thereafter Elian and his family returned to Cuba.

10

All Men Live Lives of Quiet Desperation

"All men live lives of quiet desperation."
—Henry David Thoreau

While Henry David Thoreau is often credited with varia-
tions of the saying, "Most men lead lives of quiet desperation and die with their song still inside them," that is not what he
wrote in *Walden*. He merely said, "The mass of men lead lives of
quiet desperation" (*NY Times,* April 30, 2012). I would continue
that quote with an additional "D" in reference to members of the
Witness Security Program: "All men live lives of quiet desperation
and danger."

The Program is the Program of last resort. Members of organized
crime either rot in jail for the rest of their natural life or are killed in
the street. Nobody retires with a legitimate pension or 401(k) from
their crime family. Some may squirrel away illegal funds for the
future. Very rarely does a member do jail time and then become
legitimate. True, some are able to keep ill-gotten gains; they may
have illegal gains from illegal means to sustain them for a period of

time. However, the Program provides them with a different level of protection and not just personal security.

Since most witnesses who enter the Program have criminal records, it is a difficult transformation to make from a life of crime to a legitimate life. However, ex-cons who enter the Program have a lower recidivism rate, 17 percent, than ex-cons from the general population, who have a rate of 41 percent. This is according to the Wit/Sec fact sheet. I don't know if Wit/Sec breaks down how much the government spends each year on Wit/Sec parolees in the Program. Lowering the general crime rate with a Wit/Sec style supervision would cost way too much money and there would not be enough parole officers/social workers available to make the Program successful.

Most Wit/Sec Program participants didn't live an authentic life of honesty and integrity to begin with. In their world secrets were tantamount to survival. So when they came into the Program and were told that they now must tell the truth about their past crimes… well, you can only imagine the level of anxiety they experienced. They had never publicly told the truth, and now they must not only tell the truth but they must do it publicly on a witness stand. This was painful and difficult for some. Uncomfortable, to say the least. On top of that, they are usually relocated to a state not chosen by them. Powerlessness. Now they must follow the rules and regulations of the government and of the new state, but more importantly, they have to follow the rules and regulations of the Program in WitSec World. Their road is a long transformation, and it has to begin prior to their entry into the Program. To be successful, they must be committed to undergoing a complete transformation. They must have an epiphany and become "new"!

A successful case is when they enter WitSec World and we never hear from them again, because they have assimilated into society and no longer need any services from the government. I would advise applicants for the Program to leave all their "baggage" outside the door when they come in and cross over with the government so that their future will be better than their past. Some can make the change; others cannot. Most get through with the help of their families and the government. The ones who do not make the change successfully are the ones who get thrown out, leave the Program, and get arrested, killed, or sadly take their own life.

Life in the Program is much harder than it has been depicted in TV shows or the movies. I have observed the quiet desperation of witnesses like XXX, who was on the brink of committing suicide before testifying, and of XXX, who went down that road, and the couple who died by shotgun blasts. Not all witnesses were beating the system to get a free pass on life and scamming the system by lying on the witness stand. However, that is how most are ridiculed by the defense attorneys in the defense of their clients.

I was empathetic toward witnesses and their families. The relocation Wit/Sec inspectors spent most of their time with the witnesses in their new areas. The inspector is there as a contact to assist the witness and family in the relocation process. Their position requires a totally different personality to deal with the witness and family getting settled with housing, employment, schooling, medical, and other issues. Their job is more like that of a social worker. My job was more concerned with security. I think it would be fair to say that I dealt with, interviewed, produced, and traveled with more than a hundred Witness Security Program Participants and prisoner witnesses over the years. They had to trust you to know they are in good hands. They don't care what you know. Just that they know you care about them, their family, and their unknown future.

In their former lives, they couldn't trust people. They quickly sized you up by how you handled yourself, because they were in your hands. I had to be honest with witnesses and not paint a rosy picture of their future life in the Program. Not all Program Participants are high-level criminals. Some are considered low-level street thugs, and some of these people also cooperated with the government. That is the only way the government can make cases against street gangs and drug organizations. As a result, some of the Program participants will be less than truthful in their dealings with the Marshals. That can create problems. Some Wit/Sec personnel consider some of their clients a burden. Handling them can be confrontational and exhausting. Some witnesses feel that the assistant United States attorney used them to get a feather in their cap with a conviction and then threw them away, never to be heard from again. How wrong they are!

Some witnesses who are terminated can be reinstated with the help of their sponsoring AUSA, depending on the "juice" their AUSA has with the Department of Justice. I have known cases where witnesses were terminated and relocated two and three times.

Very few organized crime cases are made without a cooperating witness. Members of organized crime who enter the Program never followed the laws of society, but they didn't follow the rules of *their* life either, because they cooperated with law enforcement. They broke their own code of silence. Just like Salvatore d'Amico in Sicily, whom I spoke of earlier. He cooperated and he warned the police that they could not protect him. In *his* life, one of the rules was that they never lie when talking family business. Many witnesses have told me they can't get over how often they have been lied to by different agents of the government—more so than when they were out on the street dealing with gangsters. On the other hand, I would hear from older witnesses that there was no more loyalty in the mob. I found it ironic that they could be cynical of the motives or virtues of other gangsters.

When they come into the Program, participants take on a life-style that some have never experienced before. Some were used to making large sums of money for a job that didn't have regular hours. Some of the underlings were expected to kick up their illegal proceeds to their captains and bosses. Now, in the Program, they are expected to get a regular job with a forty-hour workweek. Out on the street they looked at the average working man as a schmuck. While there are financial strains and boredom with many Program members, some come into the Program with large, legitimate amounts of cash. Of course, it is easier for them to live in their new area. However, others have to go to vocational schools or receive other training paid for by the government to earn a living in their relocation area.

In the late 1990s, I interviewed XXX from the New Jersey DeCavalcante crime family. XXX went into the Program with plenty of money from legitimate investments and businesses. He was a successful businessman with a definite set of skills which he decided to use in WitSec World. Rather than live under the radar, he opened a XXX. A TV show did a special about his recently opened new business and the mansion in which he lived. I don't know what happened to him and what his status is now, but I do wonder about the choice he made. It is an example of never knowing how people make that change.

The biggest adjustment for some witnesses is adjusting to what is "normal." It becomes difficult to appreciate the simple things in life. For some witnesses being relocated is like coming off a high. For others who make the change, it is like going to Disneyland, only it is called Wit/Sec World. For some it is like hitting the lottery. For others it is living a life of quiet desperation.

One of the misleading aspects of the Program is the number of witnesses who enter each year. According to the 2016 Witness

Security Fact Sheet, which is released each year, there are approximately 8,600 witnesses and 9,900 family members in the Program. Each witness has the potential to be a lifelong client. In the late 1990s, I was dealing with witnesses who had come into the Program in its inception in the 1970s. For the witness, the Program is the most hopeful of choices. It allows for redemption, a chance to cleanse their souls. Some witnesses have told me they have become religious because God does not remember the past. Many witnesses have told me the only friends they have left are the government agents they worked cases with. They lived in two worlds that were difficult and different and not easy to accept. When in "the life," witnesses had more of a chance to be killed at any time. After testifying and coming into the Program and following the rules, there was less of a chance. When on the "street," they could never know whom to trust; even their best friend might be the one sent to kill them.

Most crime stories you hear about are the arrests, trial, and acquittal or conviction and then prison. You don't hear much more after that process, nor do the movies or TV cover that period of time either. However, I look at Wit/Sec World as a truly compelling human event story. It is about people who have lived with demons. They got a break and are starting over. Everyone is entitled to the same services in the Program. It doesn't matter if you were a crime boss or street drug dealer. You are treated the same. That's 8,600 different stories and yet they all have the same dynamics.

I consider the Program to be an equal-opportunity employer. It does not matter if you are Russian, Chinese, Mexican, Colombian, Hells Angel, Arian Brotherhood, Crip or Blood, Italian, Albanian, Israeli, or from Osh Kosh. It doesn't matter if you are Catholic, Protestant, Jewish, Muslim, Buddhist, or atheist. It doesn't matter what language you speak. The Program has had participants from all walks of life: from a religious nun, to drug addicts, to crime bosses, to mass murderers, to members of Al-Qaeda. The Program can handle the needs of all those willing to make the change. As my former parish priest Father Jack once said at the end of one of his homilies, "It is all about the witnesses." And so it is.

Unfortunately, when talking about the history of the Program, I have to admit that there were some bad apples in the barrel. I am not talking about the mob now. I am talking about Wit/Sec marshals. In all my years, I knew a few who betrayed their oath of office, their fellow law enforcement officers, and the Program. Some have gotten involved with witnesses in their relocation area and involved in illegal activities. Some were arrested for gambling, lost their job, and have gone to jail. Some were arrested for stealing money from the Program. As a result, some Program procedures were changed to help alleviate certain problems. I can say without a doubt that no one in NY Metro was included in with the bad apples. I only remember talking on the phone or meeting in passing on a detail with some of them. Never did I have any dealings with them, suspect anything, or hear any rumors about their illegal activities.

Part of the trust of the position as inspector is being aware of information in indictments and the names of cooperating informants in criminal investigations. In 2007, a DUSM working a Wit/Sec detail in Chicago was charged with stealing confidential information from a Wit/Sec file that named an informant in an ongoing investigation. The marshal told a relative, who passed it on to the mob in Chicago. That marshal ended up going to prison.

11

The Al-Qaeda Case

Sometime in the fall of 1996, the new chief inspector notified me that I would be receiving a secure phone call from Headquarters. A short while later XXX, case manager, called me. She informed me that the U.S. Attorney's Office in SDNY was making a request for an interview for a terrorist case and relayed the information to me to contact them and make arrangements to interview the subject and family. I contacted AUSA Pat Fitzgerald, SDNY, and arranged to meet him at an out-of-state safe house where the FBI had the subject and family.

When I arrived, I met AUSA Fitzgerald, FBI SA Mike Anticev, and some other agents. The subject to be interviewed was XXX. He was from the Sudan, a member of al-Qaeda, and he worked directly for Osama bin Laden, looking for properties for training and buying equipment for training throughout the Middle East. He was also the payroll manager for al-Qaeda. He ripped off bin Laden and fled the Middle East with $100,000 plus and went to Europe. He knew he would be killed if found, so he walked into a U.S. embassy overseas. He said he had information on bin Laden. At that time bin Laden was named in an indictment in SDNY.

The CIA and FBI sent agents to interview him for weeks. Finally, they brought him and his family into the States. When I interviewed him, he was very cooperative and engaging. He spoke fair English, although there was an interpreter present. However, I could see there was a problem with his wife. She was very quiet and uninterested. I informed her that the Program was voluntary and if she had any issues about being relocated with her husband that she had time to think about it—it takes a while to be authorized for entry into the Program. She could make up her mind before she entered. If they and their children entered the Program and were relocated and then she decided she wanted to leave, we would have to relocate her husband so she would not know where he was. Later on without his wife knowing, XXX informed me that his wife thought a hex would be put on their family for cooperating with the U.S. government and testifying against bin Laden if he was captured and went to trial. She believed they would suffer misfortune and be killed. I informed him in front of all the other parties present of the issues of bringing someone into the Program who does not want to be relocated. This was a voluntary Program. I also informed him that since this was an unusual case of foreign aliens entering the Program, there would be additional issues of adjustment but also of assimilation in the relocation process, which would put more pressure on them and their relationship. In addition, XXX would be needed to travel to neutral sites to be prepped and debriefed for any upcoming trials besides bin Laden if there were others named in any other indictment. This would mean that his wife would be by herself with the children in a new area and in a new country. Not being able to speak English would increase her feeling of isolation.

Eventually the family was authorized and we picked up all of them and sent them on their way. As time went by, there were only a handful of people who knew about XXX's cooperation. He and his family were adjusting to their new life in their new area. His wife became pregnant and gave birth to a child who was born with a serious health problem. Now the wife was convinced that bin Laden was getting back at them for cooperating with the U.S. government. The husband had his hands full. Not only did he have anxiety about cooperating and his future testimony, something he had never done before, but he also had to hear from his distraught wife about the hex from bin Laden. What a situation! We now had a wife berating a terrorist facilitator!

In the meantime, agents and prosecutors met with XXX for debriefings in neutral sites. Agents Anticev, Dan Coleman, and Jack Cloonan would call me to discuss some of his issues. I would also meet with AUSA Fitzgerald and AUSA Ken Karas, communicate with XXX's relocation inspector, and relay the concerns. I was the liaison between the FBI Joint Terrorist Task Force, the U.S. Attorney's Office, and XXX. Over the next few months, many of his issues became very time consuming. That is not unusual in dealing with relocated witnesses. It is not a nine-to-five job. There were numerous times when I would get called about work that interrupted family or social events. Elaine would ask me, "Who was that on the phone?" I would never tell her. I would just say, "Oh, that call was about work." It was not unusual for Anticev to call me at night and ask me to meet him because he had just received photos from overseas and needed XXX to identify the subjects.

Then the two U.S. embassies were attacked in Africa by al-Qaeda on August 7, 1998. Two hundred and twenty-four people were killed. Two weeks later President Clinton ordered cruise missile strikes against the Sudan and Afghanistan. Now it was even more important for XXX to identify intel photos of suspects. This entailed more neutral site meetings. Arrests were made overseas in the bombing case, and four defendants were brought to NYC and housed at the Metropolitan Correctional Center (MCC) in lower Manhattan. At that time there was still no public information that XXX was in the U.S. and in the Program.

The trial was scheduled for the embassy bombing defendants in SDNY. XXX was terrified to testify about bin Laden and al-Qaeda. In early 2001, we produced him in court and he successfully testified about the structure of al-Qaeda as well as other involvement between al-Qaeda and bin Laden. This was a very successful continuation in law enforcement criminal prosecutions against overseas terrorism cases like the first World Trade Center bombing case.

XXX's testifying was like the first time I saw that mob trial in SDNY against Funzi Tieri being named in a RICO indictment in 1980. At the time I thought it was unique that XXX was describing the structure of al-Qaeda. It reminded me of when I first started in the job. It was just like the Italians describing the structure of the Mafia. XXX was the Joe Valachi of al-Qaeda. XXX was just as fearful as the mobsters were. However, this was a different war now. It was not like the Colombo War or other mob wars. These defendants were deliberately killing innocent Americans.

The government got convictions against all four defendants in May of 2001. Another al-Qaeda member also cooperated with the government. He was a pilot from Morocco, and testified regarding al-Qaeda's activities in Somalia. I interviewed him separately and then interviewed his wife after she was brought into the country. They also entered the Program with their children.

The terrorist war had been ongoing, and the New Year's Eve 2000 celebration of the millennium was approaching. Being proactive, AUSA Fitzgerald made a very unusual request through official channels to have quicker access to XXX. The government was concerned about a terrorist incident during the New Year's Eve celebration. As a result, secure equipment was established to communicate with XXX between New York and his relocation area. These video conferences took place between prosecutors, agents, and XXX in his new area. No longer did everyone have to travel to neutral sites.

I coordinated and sat in on all those secure video conferences with XXX. This saved time and money and was very successful for over a year.

Then there was another attack. This time in October 2000, the U.S. Navy vessel the USS *Cole* was attacked in Yemen. Seventeen U.S. sailors were killed. The war was heating up with little response by the U.S.

Around this same time, I had joined the World Trade Center Fitness Club, located on the top floor of the Vista Hotel. The hotel was between the Twin Towers. Depending on my work schedule, I would work out during the mornings or in the afternoon. One day in the locker room, I saw Dick Grasso leaving. Mr. Grasso was the CEO of the New York Stock Exchange and active with the National Italian American Foundation, of which I was a member. I didn't get a chance to introduce myself to Grasso. I wanted to because our daughter Catherine was working as a summer intern at the Stock Exchange. Catherine was going into her senior year in college. While at the exchange, she would invite me to different functions. Once she asked me to come and meet Mr. Bill Johnston, president of the exchange. Mr. Johnston was very welcoming and pleasant. We sat in his office and he explained the operation of the exchange at that time. He also gave me an autographed copy of a large coffee table book on the history of the exchange. I gave him a U.S. Marshal pin and hat. He was very pleased. We have a photo of Catherine and the other excited interns with Mr. Johnston ringing the opening bell of the exchange. That was a joyous occasion. However, the world was about to change.

At the same time I was involved with another case with the Sicilians, I met in Manhattan the following Italian officials: Dr. Guido LoForte, Dr. Antonio Ingroia, Giuseppe Ciuro, and Luigi LiGotti. They had traveled to the United States on September 10,

2001 to meet XXX in a neutral site to interview him for a deposition. LiGotti was his personal attorney. I left them at a hotel in midtown and advised them that I would meet them the next day with instructions and information on where they would be meeting with XXX.

Keeping up with my yearly medical and physical requirements, I had just the previous week randomly selected the following Tuesday to have a blood test. I scheduled it early in the morning on my way to work. That Tuesday was September 11, 2001.

After the blood test I was approaching the George Washington Bridge from Fort Lee, New Jersey, when I heard on the news that a plane had hit the Twin Towers. As I was crossing the bridge, I looked down the Hudson River and could see the smoke coming out of one of the towers. I looked in my rearview mirror and was surprised. There were no cars behind me. The Port Authority Police had shut the bridge down right behind me. They weren't allowing any vehicles to cross the bridge into New York. I tried calling on my car radio to my office, but there was no communication. We had a radio repeater on the top of the Trade Center tower. I saw all the traffic stopped heading south on the West Side. The traffic in front of me was starting to come to a stop on the New York side of the bridge. All I could see were brake lights and nowhere to go. The traffic was chaotic. I knew the Italians would be waiting in midtown.

When I reached the turnaround at the end of the bridge, I made a U-turn before going under the apartment building and the bus terminal. I went back over the bridge toward New Jersey and proceeded to a nearby police station. They gave me a desk and a phone. I tried land lines to the office but nothing worked. I also tried to contact some coworkers but couldn't. The police officers told me the second tower was also hit. I contacted the Italians and told them we would have to make other arrangements, which we did. By that time all planes were grounded.

That was the game changer. After that horrific attack, the word *security* in the United States had a new meaning. As everyone knows, downtown was devastated. The morning after the attack, I drove to work down the West Side Highway. NYPD had established a separate lane going downtown for emergency and police vehicles. I put my police sign on the dashboard and utilized that lane for weeks until the highway returned to normal. At the intersection of the West Side Highway and Canal Street, people were lined up along the highway and in the middle island waving American flags and chanting USA! USA!

When I got to my office, XXX asked me to go with him to look for his wife's government vehicle, which was parked two blocks from Ground Zero. Only official personnel were allowed in the area. We walked around searching and it was eerie. The thick dust and debris filled the streets, making them look like the surface of the moon. While we walked, we stirred up debris. There were no people on the formerly crowded streets. The air was full of smoke and an acrid smell. We found the vehicle in one piece. We didn't know if it would start or not because it was covered with so much dust that it looked like a military Humvee. It immediately started, so we cleaned it off as best as we could to see out the windows. We drove out of the area in a cloud of dust, and we were glad to be getting out of there.

The Southern District Marshals Office had a detail of personnel with appropriate equipment to help search for survivors in "the pile" at Ground Zero. The FBI Joint Terrorist Task Force moved into a garage out of the downtown area. I met with members there a few days later. They needed XXX to see some photos. Later we brought him into the tristate area, where he could be reached by prosecutors and agents within a short driving distance from the city.

Three days after 9/11, President Bush was coming to Ground Zero, which was still smoldering. Wit/Sec had been tasked with providing a security detail to the director of the Federal Emergency Management Agency, Joe Allbaugh, who would be with President Bush on Air Force One coming to New York. I was at the Wall Street heliport talking with our detail personnel, awaiting the arrival of the President's detail, when I saw Lt. Jerry Sheehan, commanding officer of the NYPD bomb squad. Jerry didn't live too far from me. We spoke about the disaster, the loss of life, and how it would impact our future. There was a huge law enforcement presence around Ground Zero that day.

After 9/11 a major shift in manpower assignments at the FBI was an indication of how things had changed. In the 1980s the FBI had criminal squads of agents assigned to each organized crime (OC) family. After 9/11 the numbers of OC squads were basically cut in half. It is no secret that more agents were reassigned to terrorism, cybersecurity, and other related investigations.

The last big OC case was XXX, the boss of the Bonnano family. He was referred to as the last of the Dons. He was convicted of murder in 2004. I never had any contact with him, and all I know about him is what I heard or read in the papers.

Today there aren't as many mob murders as before. One reason is that the leaders want to settle disputes. They do not want members facing long jail times for murder, which could lead to their members making deals with the government and cooperating. The passage of the RICO laws and the establishment of the Witness Security Program severely punished La Cosa Nostra in the United States over the last forty years.

XXX's defection alone accounted for more than fifty convictions in numerous trials in different districts. He also cooperated with other prosecutors in other cities around the country. and was invited to speak at an FBI seminar. Besides other topics he told agents how to effectively deal with cooperating witnesses.

After 9/11 everything was turned upside down and the government was reorganizing. The war on OC and the mob in America was very successful but it was not complete. In the 1990s, working on XXX's case opened my eyes to the new war the government would be involved in. In order to defeat terrorism, the public would have to overcome the fear factor in changing our social norms, which is almost impossible to do and may take a very long time, especially when soft targets are attacked. From the first World Trade Center bombing and the embassy bombings to the attack on the USS *Cole*, it was evident who had the upper hand. These are examples of the types of targets to be attacked. A soft target, a hardened target, and a military target. There was no real push back from our government. Al Qaeda was the new mob. It was the equivalent of the 1950s era of the government not responding to, acknowledging, or fighting the mob.

The days of the rough and tough gangster are over. In the movies and in real life, the paint on that painting has dried. The old mobsters have been dying off. There are very few left who have the historical insight, relevant information of criminal activities, or status in the mob. As a result, the number of witnesses entering the Program has declined. That reflects on the Program adapting to the new order. The Program wasn't created to just accept Italian mobsters. As I pointed out earlier, the Program is an equal opportunity employer. For example, a *New York Times* article of May 17, 2013 stated: "The Justice Department temporarily lost track of two former terrorists who had participated in its witness protection Program and until recently did not disclose the fictitious identities it created for terrorism-linked witnesses to the agency that generates watch lists, allowing some who were on the no-fly list to take commercial flights under their new names, according to a new report." This is an example of how the Program has to understand its responsibilities in a changing new world and adjust its procedures accordingly.

My time to retire was approaching. When I had returned a survivor from the motor vehicle accident in Arizona, I told Elaine in 1996 that I would leave in five years. Fifty-seven was the mandatory retirement age, after the government raised it from fifty-five, for law enforcement personnel. The government wanted to retain experienced personnel. When I was preparing to transition into retirement, I called the relocation inspector to inform him I was leaving and that Inspector XXX in New York would now be his contact for all of XXX's needs, including the video conferences. During that conversation, the relocation inspector asked me, "What should I do with the tapes?"

"What tapes?" I asked.

I was shocked. I was not aware that the secure video conferences were being recorded. He told me he had been recording the meetings I had sat in between XXX and the prosecutors and agents.

I told him, "I don't know anything about those tapes or being recorded, but someone will be in touch with you."

Sometime later, I had a conversation with Branch Chief XXX, Wit/Sec Headquarters. We discussed that however many tapes there were, they had to be turned over to the U.S. Attorney's office as discovery material for the defense attorneys in the case XXX testified in. These tapes included debriefings about the case and preparations for XXX's testimony for upcoming trials. There were also discussions with him about his issues in the Program. Notes were taken by the agents and prosecutors during the video conferences. XXX from Headquarters asked me to notify AUSA Pat Fitzgerald. I called Pat and advised him of the taping. His response was "Oh shit!" I later received a call from XXX from Headquarters who informed me that Wit/Sec had to go through the tapes and redact any security information and turn them over to the Office of Enforcement Operations and the U.S. Attorney's Office, SDNY.

I retired and never heard anything else officially from anyone about the tapes. I started a new job as a contract investigator for the FBI and the U.S. State Department. I read a short article in the *New York Times* on January 23, 2004 which read, "Three Seek Retrial in Bombing of Embassies." The lawyers for the al-Qaeda members convicted in the U.S. embassy bombing case filed for a new trial, citing a number of issues, including not knowing about the video-taping with XXX and the written notes. All four defendants were serving life in prison.

On February 18, 2004, another article in the *Times* was "U.S. Judge Sees Stonewalling on Tapes in Terrorism Case." I picked up the *New York Times* on May 1, 2004 and read the front-page head-line: "U.S. Videos of Qaeda Informer Offer Glimpse into a Secret Life." The *Times* also ran another larger article in their December 9, 2007 Sunday edition, "How to Keep an Ex-Terrorist Talking."

In May 2005, my mother had just passed away a few days earlier when I received a call at home from AUSA Dave Raskin, SDNY, who informed me that Judge Duffy was holding hearings about the video conference tapes and I would be needed to testify. He wanted to talk to me in his office about this incident. I met with him on May 25, 2005 and briefed him on my position, purpose, and presence at the video conferences with XXX. He questioned me about some of the facts. I informed him I had no knowledge those sessions were being taped in the relocation area.

On June 7, 2005, I testified in the hearing before Judge Duffy in U.S. District Court, 40 Foley Square in Manhattan. I again denied any knowledge of the taping. One of the legal issues was if Wit/Sec was part of the prosecution team. While on the witness stand, AUSA Raskin asked me what my role was during the secure video confer-ence sessions. I stated that I was present to make sure there was no breach of security of XXX's relocation area among other things. I was also questioned by the defense attorney about my role. I explained I was there for security reasons and maintaining the video conference equipment. Of course, I took no notes of the conversations nor did I record any of the session. I was on the stand for about thirty minutes.

In November 2005, Judge Duffy issued an Opinion and Order denying the motion for a new trial. However, the judge blasted the Marshals Service. "Through a mixture of inaction, incompetence, and stonewalling to cover up their mistakes, the United States Marshals Service and the Department of Justice's Office of Enforcement Operations have seriously jeopardized the convictions of al Qaeda terrorist Wadih El-Hage." As far as I know, no action was taken against any Wit/Sec personnel.

When I first heard about the tapes, I was devastated. It was an embarrassment. I knew it was going to be a black eye for Wit/Sec. I never asked anyone in Wit/Sec who ordered the relocation inspector to videotape those sessions. I didn't suspect the inspector of doing it on his own, and he never mentioned it to me prior to the telephone call when I was getting ready to retire. I can't answer for him but he should have known better.

Over the years NY Metro has had a very good reputation within the law enforcement community, the courts, and the witnesses. I had been working closely for years with many of the assistant U.S. attorneys in SDNY, EDNY, and D/NJ on many different cases. For five years I worked on this case with XXX. There was never a major issue that couldn't be resolved or fire that we couldn't put out. I had developed a good relationship with FBI Agents Mike Anticev, Dan Coleman, Jack Cloonan, and many others from the Joint Terrorism Task Force. Mike had talked to me at one point about going to the Middle East with them. They were going to approach someone they were targeting and wanted me to be able to explain the Program to this person overseas. This way they wouldn't have to bring the person into the States in case the person declined the Program. I told them I did not think Washington would approve it. It never materialized. The agents went overseas and brought me back a nameplate in Arabic for my desk.

I did not expect to walk out the door with this taping incident hanging over me, NY Metro, and Wit/Sec. I always told other inspectors that the only publicity the Program gets is bad press when something goes wrong. It was not like the Enforcement Division with the Warrant Squad. They thrived on publicity in making arrests, being on TV in local and national news. They were overt while we were covert.

NY Metro was always a good place to work. The office had a good reputation within Wit/Sec and the service, the result of the hard work and dedication of personnel who worked there over the years since the start of the Program. Most influential was the late XXX, who was instrumental in getting New York Metro operating in a professional manner. And, of course, there was XXX, who followed XXX and continued the legacy. I only wish I could recognize by name all the personnel who worked there from the start, but you know who you are. Thank you.

12

Cooking

"Eating is not merely a material pleasure. Eating well gives a spectacular joy to life and contributes immensely to goodwill and happy companionship. It is of great importance to the morale."

—Elsa Schiaparelli

The one universal topic frequently discussed with witnesses was food. It didn't matter if you were eating with them, driving in a car, or flying on a plane. The one topic that was always discussed was your all-time favorite meal. Sometimes, depending on the characters, it was even what your request would be for your last meal!

Some of the witnesses shared their favorite recipes with me; others wrote them down and gave them to me. I exchanged my mother's recipe for her Sicilian *froscia*. My mother told me her mother would always make this because it was quick and easy. Like a frittata, it is just eggs, cheese, bread crumbs, garlic, and fresh mint. It should have the consistency of a heavy pancake mix. Then it is fried in olive oil until golden brown. My mother would fold it and flip it like an omelet. I make it in little batches. Our whole family still makes our mother's pizza, meatballs, and sauce. When growing up, our mother would make pizza from scratch for us on our birthdays. Everyone loved it! We also still make my father's favorite: polenta with sausages and blue cheese. Over the years on the anniversaries of their birthdays, we would have the family over to our house to enjoy once again our parents' favorite dishes. Recently, it has been difficult since some travel to Florida for the winter months while others are relocated in other states. But we make up for it.

In Nanny Down's house there was always a wonderful aroma of food simmering on the stove. It might be the sauce or the chicken or the veal cutlets. No matter what it was, it was always the best! Sometimes I walk into an Italian store and catch a whiff that transports me back to my nanny's, an experience I realized that many of the witnesses will not have in their new locations. They will only have the memories of what used to be.

There was also a kitchen in Nanny's basement that included a huge, long country dining table. Many Sunday dinners were enjoyed at that table. After dinner, space was made for music and singing. My grandmother would play her tambourine and make up Sicilian folk songs. That tambourine has been handed down to my brother Sal, who continued to use it when he sang at his local church. Aunt Jo, the Franciscan nun, also sang. She had a beautiful voice and sang "Sorrento" at my wedding when I married Elaine.

My uncle Charlie played the violin and Aunt Angie Beebe played the piano. She traveled up from Philadelphia with her sons, Michael and George. My mother told me I was named after Aunt Angie's husband, George Beebe. We referred to him as Uncle Ski. He was tall and the manager of the Drexel Hill Country Club outside of Philadelphia. He had many celebrity friends, including Ed McMahon and Dick Clark. My sister Jacque, cousins, and friends would be invited to appear on the popular TV show *American Bandstand*. Aunt Angie was very classy. She went on to become the secretary for a United States District Court judge in Philadelphia for many years until she retired.

On special Sundays we would visit Aunt Jo at the convent in Peekskill and the St. Joseph's Orphanage. We never knew what color her hair was because of the veil covering her hair and head. We would try to get close to see if we could see any evidence of her hair showing. In the early 1970s while in the military, I was in Phoenix visiting the Sollomis. Theresa showed me a photo and said, "Do you know who this is?"

It was Aunt Jo. She was in civilian clothes. That was the first time I had ever seen her hair and did not know she had just left the Franciscans because of health reasons.

When Aunt Jo, Sister Inez, was allowed to go home, she would bring some of the nuns with her. Going to my grandparents' house at that time was like a retreat. Nanny Down would take very good care of them. She would also tell them to take naps in the bedrooms and cover them with blankets. Her kindness extended to anyone who entered her house. They would eat, drink, and enjoy themselves. Over the years I have met some of those same nuns, who raved about the food and the memories. They would tell me how my grandparents were very special people. And my mother? She was in the kitchen doing the dishes!

My family never did the traditional Italian feast of the seven fishes on Christmas Eve. However, my mom would make whiskey balls! She put whiskey inside dough and fried them. As we grew older we could never understand how she did it because you would only taste the whiskey when you took a bite out of the middle of the dough.

When I was growing up, I was always intrigued by the way my mother cooked. She always had an ongoing grocery list that continued to get longer and longer as she thought about the day's meals. When she felt it was complete, she would call the Hub Market with her order and she would pay them monthly. They delivered boxes of food to the back door. I would help carry food in and put it away with her. The veal cutlets from the Hub were one inch thick then. We still talk about how tender they were. When she cooked, I would patiently watch her add a little of this and a little of that. She would always tell me to drink the real milk. After all, she grew up on goat's milk. I appreciated her efforts as I got older and signed up for my first cooking lesson. That was in the late 1970s when I was a member of the cultural organization called the Italy-America Society at 667 Madison Avenue. After taking some basic classes, I would watch her hands as she cooked. I was amazed how she cut garlic. She never used a cutting board to peel and smash the garlic. She would put a clove in the palm of her hand and take a small knife and peel and cut the garlic into tiny pieces in her hands!

On December 13th, St. Lucy Day, my grandmother would make *cuccia*. Her daughter Rosy had an eye ailment, and my grandmother prayed to St. Lucy that if she fixed her daughter's eyes, she would make this dish every December 13th. Rosie's eyes recovered and we all ate *cuccia*! It was composed of wheat, white beans, garlic, and olive oil. She soaked the beans overnight. Then she fried them in the oil and added the garlic. It is made differently in each town in Sicily. Some even add chocolate.

When my mother passed away in 2005, Catherine, our older daughter, wrote the following and printed it out. A large number of copies were placed at the reception sign-in table at the wake for my mother at the funeral home. The people who came to pay their respects took a copy. People kept asking the funeral home for more copies. I have another photo of Catherine and Theresa mixing dough. They are in the same spot my mother is in our kitchen using the same wooden board. This letter is a priceless memory. It represents Catherine and Theresa's best memory of their nanny in the kitchen.

NANNY'S CUCINA: YOU EITHER EAT TO LIVE, OR LIVE TO EAT.

Being a Dapra, I have never been deprived of good rustic meals. I have learned from the best, and developed this certain passion that many Italians have about food and eating. Nanny was always focused on the next meal...

My dad used to say, "Ma, you've been to the Grand Union three times today!" and Nanny always said she didn't know what she was having for dinner at 11am. I never understood it either until I started cooking and realized you won't know what you really need until you need it! This became a life lesson learned in the kitchen. Nanny made everything with love, passion and whole milk.

I remember Nanny's cooking: the way that Mearns Ave smelled when she sautéed her garlic and oil, to walk into the kitchen and find her smooth cheeks as rosy as her tomato sauce, and to be amazed that my itty bitty grandmother could reach her oversized aluminum pots to stir in her love.

For me, the most memorable reminder of home is scent. I can close my eyes and remember all the fragrances, tastes and textures of Nanny's pizzas, meatballs, froscia (a secret family recipe). Nanny lived to cook and share her food with everyone.

To remember her passion and spirit, we would like to share one of her recipes with you.

Another Pizza with Jennie...

5lbs flour
3 pkgs. Yeast
Warm water and a pinch of salt
Sauce: crushed tomatoes, garlic, oregano, parmesan

Pour the flour and make a well in the middle. Add the yeast, a cup of warm water, and a pinch of sugar and salt. Add more water as needed. Mix together, kneading gently, and let it rise in a very large pot with a dishtowel over the top. Place the pot on top of your radiator. When it has risen to the top of the pot, it's ready (this can take up to 4hrs).
Knead it some; roll it out lightly with flour; and cover it with crushed tomatoes, sea salt, oregano and garlic. Add some parmesan cheese and olive oil and cook in a very hot oven (approx. 500 degrees) for 8-10 minutes or until lightly golden brown.
Enjoy with family and friends! Mangia!

All of my love, Catherine

In the cellar of my grandparents' house was a cabinet with a turntable that played the original 33 and 78 rpm records. Today, I have that old Brunswick Panatrope by RCA and those heavy, thick records from various Italian and American singers on Columbia, Victor, and Etna records. Sometimes when I used to walk through Chinatown and Little Italy, I would encounter a funeral procession of a few elderly men playing their instruments and the sour music, and I would think of those old records. At times, I still play my grandfather's records of Nicola Paone, who later owned a restaurant by the same name near 34th Street and Third Avenue. Today, the restaurant is empty and so is that cellar. My grandparents' house is now a multi-family residence. In the past that cellar would come to life with laughter and music. All the grownups spoke Italian. Sometimes when my brothers and sisters were playing outside I just liked to sit in the corner and listen to the grownups talk and carry on. They wanted us to grow up speaking English, get an American education and a good job. When they wanted us kids to go outside and play, they would give my oldest brother Larry money to march us down to the movie theater. That was good training for him because he ended up graduating from West Point and making a career in the military.

Being a first-generation Italian-American, I could speak to some of these witnesses and relate to their stories, family situations, and recipes. Some would tell me that you can't get good Italian bread or pizza outside of New York. We would talk about how the water and humidity make a difference in New York. Also, the water for New York City travels down from the Catskill Mountains through a tremendous inventive aqueduct system built in the 1800s. That water from the mountains is rich in minerals. However, today it is possible to get good pizza and bread in towns and cities outside of New York. I also could relate to what many witnesses would miss once they made their commitment to enter the Program and to begin a new life, in a new area, with their memories holding them together.

After a few years and many discussions, I thought I would collect some of the recipes from some of the characters I dealt with in the Program.

Very rarely would Elaine call me at work. However, one day she did reach me and asked, "Can you bring home a loaf of the provolone bread from Little Italy"?

"Of course." There was an elderly Italian man in the back of the Italian Food Center on Grand Street who would make the bread. I would talk to him about how he made it. One winter day I had bought a loaf. It started snowing when I was getting ready to leave work. I got stuck on the FDR in traffic for over an hour. I reached into the bag with the bread and started breaking off pieces and eating while stuck in traffic. By the time I got home there were only crumbs left!

In another phone conversation, Elaine asked me how I was doing. I responded, "Fine, I am just exchanging recipes."

Elaine said, "Oh, with some of the girls in the office?"

"NO! With some of the mobsters!"

I told the witnesses that someday I would write a book about mob recipes. They agreed that it was a good idea and said I could use their recipes.

Here are a few:

When I asked XXX to write down his favorite, he told me to write down his recipe and then he signed the paper it was on.

XXX was a captain in the XXX crime family. He was close to the boss XXX. XXX was involved in the XXX and labor activities. He told the government how XXX was the real boss of the family.

This recipe is a cold potato salad. After he gave me the recipe, he told me he even likes it with a little celery in it and you can add anything else you like. I made it for him with celery and we shared it one night while he was in town to testify against John Gotti.

Small Red Potatoes
Garlic
Oil
Mint
S + P
Parsley
Peas?
Red Pepper

Boil Potatoes. Wash cold water.
In Dish Slice Garlic/oil.
Add Mint Leaves.
Slice Potatoes in half.
Add Potato dish. Add pepper, parsley, red pepper.
Add Peas. Cover. Place in Refrigerator Over night.
Eat cold.

XXX was a con man and Wall Street swindler. XXX owned restaurants in the Boston area, Miami, and New York. He told me he liked the following quick recipe for fresh fish that he would make at home.

Any Filet oF Fish - I like
Northern Tish - Cod, Haddock, Sole
make Sure completely de boned -

Grind up Ritz crackers Fine
like Bread crumbs

Dip Fish Filet in either vegetable
or olive oil + Than Dip IN Ritz cracker
crumbs - So top of Filet is completely
Covered.
Place on sheet Pan put 1/2 inch
of Combination water + milk on pan -
(Do Not cover Tish) + place pat of
Butter on Tish + Bake until Tish is
Done - About 20 minutes

XXX was the XXX. After he cooperated, he was housed in a XXX where he became the cook for the other witnesses. When we talked about food, he was very interested in healthy foods and a healthy lifestyle. A few years ago, a part of his life was portrayed in the movie XXX.

DELICIOUS CHEESE BURGER

2 STALKS CELERY
2 ONIONS (SMALL)
2 EGG
4 SLICES CHEESE
1 TABLESPOON CHICKENBASE
1 TABLE SPOON SWEET BASIL
1 TABLESPOON WORCESTERSHIRE SAUCE
5 TABLESPOONS

FINELY CHOP CELERY + ONIONS. PLACE IN PAN
WITH TWO BEATEN EGGS. MIX THIS WITH, CHICKEN
BASE, BASIL, WORCESTERSAIRE SAUCE. WHEN
MIXTURE IS SMOOTH THEN KNEAD THIS INTO MEAT.
SHAPE MEAT TO SIZE. COOK 25 MIN., OR TO
PREFERENCE. TURN OFF OVEN PUT CHEESE
ON AND REPLACE IN TURNED OFF OVEN UNTIL
CHEESE IS MELTED

CANDIED SWEETS

SWEET POTATOES, THINLY SLICED ORANGES (WITH SKIN))
MELTED BUTTER, MOLASSES. PLACE, SLICED
TO PREFERENCE, SWEETS IN PAN. PUT ORANGE
SLICES ON SWEETS, POUR ON RESONABLE BUTTER.
SPRINKLE WITH BROWN SUGAR + SALT MIXTURE.
BAKE ABOUT 20 MIN; BASTE WITH MOLASSES, BAKE
20 MINUTES LONGER.

GREENS

VINEGAR
BROWN SUGAR
GROUND CLOVES
ONIONS
GREEN PEPPER
GARLIC

COOK GREENS IN VERY SHALLOW WATER (1/2 HR.)
MIX IN GARLIC (6 PIECES), CHOPPED GREEN
PEPPER + ONION, GROUND CLOVES, VINEGAR (TABLE
SPOON), COOK 30 MIN.

XXX was a Sicilian drug dealer and a local chef in a New York restaurant. This was his favorite Bolognese sauce recipe. Once I had to put him on a flight out of New York. I bought his ticket in the name of Mario D. Cook.

FOR 6
BOLOGNESE SAUCE
GARLIC, ONION, CELERY, CARROT, GRRHND MEAT
CHICKEN SOUP, RED WINE, SALT, PEPPER, BASEL
OLIVE OIL, TOMATOP (NO FRESH TOMATOS SQUEEZED)

½ CUP OIL (SOTE)
GALIC (3) SMASH   1/31/0
ONION, CELLERY, CARROT LET SUTE
MEAT (SOTE)
1 GRASS RED WINE LET COOK FOR
5 MINUTE
1 CUP CHICKEN SOUP LET COOK DR SLOWLY
PUT THE TOMATO AFTER 1 HOUR
PUT THE SPICES

LOW FLAME (COOK) 1 MORE HR.

XXX, a Sicilian who was arrested on drug charges in Miami, testified in XXX in an unusual case in XXX. As a result of the Mafia war in Sicily and the bombings that killed Judge Falcone and Borsellino, the Italian government requested that an Italian trial be held in XXX because of security concerns in Sicily. XXX testified about the relationship between the Colombians and Sicilians in the drug trade. I produced XXX for depositions with the Italian authorities.

COTOLETTE ALLA PARMIGGIANA

INGRIDIENTS FOR 4 PORTIONS.

4 SLICES OF VEAL CUTLETS (LEG CUT TOP ROUND)
   $\frac{1}{2}$" INCH THICK APPROX. SIZE 7"X 4".
1 CUP OF PLAIN BREAD CRUMBS .
$\frac{1}{4}$ LB OF GREATED IMPORTED PARMESAN CHEESE (PARMA)
$\frac{1}{2}$ BUNCH OF CHOPPED FRESH PARSLEY (USE OTHER HALF TO
   GARNISH EACH SERVING)
4 CLOVES OF FRESH GARLIC CHOPPED REAL FINE
3 LARGE FRESH TOMATOES (REMOVE SKIN & SEEDS) CHOPPED.
6 CAPERS CHOPPED VERY FINE .
4 JUMBO EGGS
— SALT & PEPPER TO YOUR TASTE.

MIX BREAD CRUMBS WITH $\frac{1}{4}$ LB OF PARMESAN CHEESE & HALF
OF THE AMOUNT OF CHOPPED PARSLEY & GARLIC , SALT &
PEPPER TO YOUR TASTE. BEAT 4 EGGS, DIP EACH CUTLET
INTO THE EGGS, DRAIN, NEXT TO BE BREADED & FRIED IN
HOT OLIVE OIL, 3 MINUTES ON ONE SIDE, 2 MINUTES ON
THE OTHER . DRAIN & WIPE YOUR FRYING PAN , USE
2 TABLESPOON OF OLIVE OIL & STIR FRYE , FOR
ABOUT 5 MINUTES THE CHOPPED TOMATOES , REMAINING
CHOPPED GARLIC, PARSLEY, CAPERS, ADD SALT & PEPPER TO
YOUR TASTE. DIVIDE TOMATOES SAUCE IN 4 EQUAL PARTS
& SPREAD ON EACH SLICE OF CUTLET, & SPRINKLE
THE PARMESAN CHEESE ON TOP.
                    BUON APPETITO

Epilogue

The environment in NYC in 1980 was tense. After the fiscal crises of the mid-seventies and high crime rates, the city was struggling. It was not lost but was crawling back out of the gutter. Forget politics. No matter if you liked them or not, Giuliani and Bloomberg restored the city to world status. I considered myself very lucky to be at the right time and the right place in my career in federal law enforcement in SDNY. It was a growth period both for the U.S. Marshals, the Wit/Sec Program, and New York City.

On the opposite side, it was the years of the decline of the mob. It wasn't just the creation of the Program and the RICO laws that helped fight the war against organized crime; it was also the right choices that were being made by the cooperators entering the Program. Some had no choice; some tried to play the system to get a break or a reduction in their sentence for cooperating. Some saw the light and did the math. They would never see the outside of a prison again for the rest of their lives.

Do you remember hearing about or seeing Joe Valachi on TV? Valachi was arrested in the 1960s for narcotics violation. He agreed to cooperate and testified at a U.S. Senate hearing in Washington about organized crime. At the time these hearings and his testimony were news worthy. This was the first high-profile mobster to report publicly about organized crime in America prior to the creation of the Program. A special prison suite was created for Valachi, who passed away in the early 1970s. In the late 1980s another marshal and I went out to that prison to bring a protected prisoner witness back to New York. The inmate had been living in the "Valachi Suite," which at that time was still being used for certain inmates. Today, I do not know if that cell still exists.

No longer were the five crime families in NYC as strong as they were in the 1970s to the 1990s. Their leadership has changed and they are now referred to as "Oldfellas" instead of "Goodfellas." They have reverted to the same tactic I referred to earlier in this book about the mob boss Funzi Tieri being wheeled into the court-room with a nurse. Today it is all about their health problems. Some of the men and women in law enforcement I worked with often re-mind me how fortunate we were to be there in NYC at that time in the battle to fight organized crime.

I have described some of the details and cases that I worked dur-ing my years there. My coworkers in the Wit/Sec office weren't sitting around. They also were involved in other high-profile cases, not only in the New York area but also throughout the U.S. and other countries overseas. These included protective details of Program witnesses who testified in cases in Greece, Israel, England, Puerto Rico, and special details in Colombia, Central America, and the Olympic Games. I had a good working relationship with Wit/Sec managers in Headquarters. Some were former coworkers in SDNY and NY Metro who made that move to Washington. I stayed because I enjoyed my position in the field in NY Metro. Those managers I often spoke with would inform me of traveling overseas to speak at international conferences about Witness Security. Other countries wanted to learn from our success.

For those who made the right choices and entered the Program, who hung on to that life preserver, realized that their past failures were not fatal. I witnessed how organized crime destroyed many lives on both sides in the war. It was not glamorous. When friends or family would talk about how good a certain mob movie was, I would just shake my head. The real-life participants knew how ruthless some of the players were. It was not easy for someone to make that choice to enter the Program. It was about separation. It was about fear. It was about not knowing what the future will be.

During my first interview of that Hells Angel guy who wanted to bring his red truck, I saw firsthand the agony of making that decision to join the Program. He was very upset that he couldn't bring his truck with him into his new relocation area. However, I realized over time that his reaction wasn't really about not being able to bring the truck. It was his first taste of the sacrifices—what he would have to give up for a new life in the Program. That red truck was a symbol of his former life and all he would have to leave behind. Sure, he could bring his memories with him, but he could not nor should he try to duplicate that red truck in his new relocation area. He faced that moment of realization earlier than most. He was only in the preliminary stage of a long journey. He was just taking his first steps. From my experience, it hits some people when they leave where they were living or when they arrive in their new relocation area. Most people are fearful of change. We are creatures of habit. With people entering the Program, they have the added fear and danger of their lives being threatened. If they had no faith in the future, then they would have no power in the present to make that change.

The same Witness Security Program that was offered equally to all applicants realized different results. Some took advantage of the life-saving situation by making a change and not getting involved in new criminal activity. They assimilated into society in a new area with a new identity with the assistance of the government. That is what the purpose of the Program is all about.

Others experienced bleak days and out of desperation couldn't make the change and took their own lives. Some resorted to their old criminal ways and were either killed in the commission of a crime or ended up back in prison. Some even return to their old ways and reconnect with friends. Everyone and every case is different. It was unfortunate that they were not able to make the pilgrimage toward true redemption like the majority of witnesses do. In reality they were slaves of the criminal world. They were rudderless, driven by a gale force wind. Their last condition was worse than their first. They had an opportunity for change that they failed to grasp. What happened to them is expressed in Proverbs 26:11: "The dogs return to their own vomit, so a fool repeats his folly."

Being a first-generation Italian-American, I can relate to this sacrifice of change. My parents came to this country with only their clothes on their back but with their memories intact. They did not need to live in fear. They were young when their parents brought them to this country. The parents were the ones who had to make the sacrifice of change. They were the ones who were leaving family and friends. They cut ties with their church, community, and close connections. I am sure they all missed their Sunday dinner ritual with their family back in their hometown as much as I miss mine of my childhood.

My journey was most rewarding. However, I learned early in my law enforcement career about the sacrifices I would have to make as a father and as a husband. As I mentioned earlier in this book, in the first couple of years I was not able to witness the birth of my first daughter or be at the bedside of my dying father. I would place those events as milestones in one's lifetime. Then, I experienced the near fatal and almost life-crippling vehicle accident in Arizona. I believe that experience was a wakeup call in my world at the time to stop and smell the roses.

After I recuperated in the hospital and was being released, the nurses showed me my belongings. I told them to throw away my cut-up clothes. The only item I kept was my wristwatch, which I never wore again. To this day I never wear a watch.

I am very grateful to the people who hired me for the different positions I held over the years, especially Jack Brophy and XXX, who are both former U.S. Marines. I am also proud to have worked with other Italian-Americans in positions of trust. I think I upheld my responsibilities and my oath to defend the Constitution of the United States. My family values are Italian; my civic values are American. From my family and work experiences I learned first-hand about the struggle between assimilation and the preservation of one's cultural birthright.

Since the 1970s when I discovered and explored more of my Italian-American heritage, I joined many Italian organizations, in-cluding Club Trentino of New York, the National Italian American Foundation (NIAF), and the American Italian Heritage Association in Albany, New York. I have gone to several NIAF annual week-end galas in Washington, D.C. On Friday night they would have a grappa and cigar bar set up in the hotel. USMS personnel from our headquarters would meet me there. Every year NIAF would honor celebrities. One of my best memories was when Tony Bennett set up his combo to sing a special love song to Sophia Loren, who was one of the honorees. Robert De Niro was also on the stage that night.

One year Elaine accompanied me to one of the events, and an-other year our daughter Catherine also attended. NIAF also had a special Program for Italian-American students, the Gift of Discovery Program, which was a two-week, all-expense-paid trip to Italy. The students would meet other Italian-American students and partake in cultural tours and activities. During one of the first years of the Program, Catherine was selected for the trip. She still keeps in touch with some of the other Italian-American students she met on her adventure. Catherine was also selected for a college scholarship from the National Law Enforcement Foundation, which honors the students at a yearly luncheon at the Waldorf Astoria that I used to attend. She now works for a New York law firm.

Our other daughter, Theresa, grew up being a champion step dancer. She won trophies as tall as she was. She is a fashionista and artist. Among other endeavors, she has created headpieces for Lady Gaga for many of her appearances. She works for an artist with studios and galleries in New York and Miami. I am very proud of both of them and love them very much.

I had a good run. I enjoyed going to work. In July of 2000, I went to a retirement seminar for a couple of days in Washington, D.C. When I returned home and spoke with Elaine, we decided I would work one more year as originally planned. January was usually the best time to retire for different reasons. I had to leave at age fifty-seven, which was mandatory. Working the case with XXX in the late nineties, I knew we were in a war with al Qaeda. Only a few months after 9/11, I would be out the door. A big change was coming to the way government operated. I counted my blessings in working Wit/Sec and dealing with the OC characters. I didn't consider myself quitting in the middle of a fight. There wasn't a call-to-arms moment. The mob had been crippled by all the convictions during the 1980s and 1990s in SDNY, EDNY, and the D/NJ.

I had been exploring other options after retirement. When I retired in January of 2002, I went to work for the U.S. Department of State and the FBI as a special investigator, working as a federal contractor. I maintained my top-secret security clearance and continued to have my five-year update reinvestigation conducted by the government until 2015.

In early 2012, Tommy Dades, retired NYPD homicide detective, contacted me about a TV show he was putting together about the Colombo War and witnesses who were in the Program. Tommy worked on a federal task force when I first met him in the 1990s. I interviewed a witness on a case he was working, and he asked me to represent the Program in the show. I told him I didn't want to get involved with any hatchet job or any show that shed bad light on the Program. He told me that was not going to be the case with the script he was planning. He said he had lined up four or five former Wit/Sec witnesses who were on board to be interviewed for the show. After some additional discussions I told Tommy I would think about it and to let me know what it was all about. During the next few months Tommy called and updated me with any new developments on his attempts to pitch the show to production companies.

One day in July I received a call from Tommy, who asked me to come to his house in a few days. He had made arrangements with two producers from Hollywood who were taking the red-eye flight in from Los Angeles and going to his house to talk about the show. He told me they wanted to interview us.

On Friday July 20, 2012, I drove to Tommy's house, where I met Matt Renner from Undertow Productions, one of the producers of the successful Discovery channel show *Deadliest Catch*. Also with Renner was Jensen Noyes. Renner explained what they wanted to do for that day and what we were going to do for the weekend. Later we drove around and showed them some crime scene locations and social clubs connected to the Colombo war, which took place in the early 1990s. They filmed us at some spots. Then we stopped at houses where the former witnesses were located. Renner then briefed them on what was going to happen over the weekend.

On Saturday we met Ethan Prochnik, another Undertow producer. Undertow had rented out an Italian restaurant in Westchester

County for the day for the filming of the pitch for the show. A large round table was set up where the witnesses, Tommy, and I sat. They discussed events that happened back in the 1990s. Sitting next to me was Linda Scarpa Schiro, daughter of the late Colombo capo Greg Scarpa. Linda was walking out of the house with a young child when the failed attempted assassination and shootout with Greg Scarpa took place. This incident and many more that took place during the Colombo war have been described in other books. Some of those shooters were former Program members sitting at the table. This was the first time she ever met face-to-face with them. It was a very dramatic and intense scene when they confronted one another. At one point, Linda leaned over to me and said, "I am the Deadliest Catch!" After a few months Tommy called me to say none of the networks picked up the show.

On a more personal note, when I retired from the Marshals, my mother was still living with my sister Jacque and her family, in the house we grew up in. My mother started getting dementia, and other medical issues arose. She couldn't be left alone at her age in her early nineties. Prior to this time period she rarely went into a hospital. Once she even told me that the last time she was in the hospital was when I was born. Finally, we had to make arrangements for her to be placed in a nearby nursing home. Since I had just retired I was more than willing to assist my mother in making the end of her life more comfortable even if it meant going into a nursing home. She did not complain. For a while she was able to get around and use a walker. We put a basket and a little kid's bike horn on it for her because she was still very active in the nursing home. Even with her own medical issues, she continued being her loving and caring self, helping the nurses. She was forever walking up and down the halls, checking on the other patients. She would even make their beds for them. They all loved her. She never complained about anything right up to the end of her life. During her last few days, I would stay with her at her bedside.

One afternoon a middle-aged man arrived at the nursing home and said he was from hospice. He wanted to know if my mother wanted someone to sit with her to keep her comfortable. He had read my mother's file and saw that she was born in Sicily. Well, he went on to say he used to live in the Bronx, and his neighbor was in the Mafia.

I said, "Wow, is that right. Why don't you leave? You are insulting and don't stop in to see my mother again."

He looked at me, didn't say a word, and left. I was upset and later told Elaine and my brother Lee to let me know if they ever saw that guy again. Looking back, I am struck by what a strange encounter that was! A few days later my mother passed away at the age of ninety-four.

In 2016, I experienced the heartbreaking death of another beloved family member. Late one night I received a phone call from an EMT worker. He advised me that Aunt Josephine, the ex-nun, had passed away in her sleep. I had spoken to her by phone twice earlier that same day. She told me she was tired but okay. After I received that call, I couldn't go back to sleep that night. I poured myself a glass of scotch and started writing her obituary and stayed up till dawn. Soon I would have to start calling to notify relatives and others of our loss.

I thought about my older family members who had gone before. Josephine was the youngest. She was the last of her generation in our family. No longer would I have anyone to call an aunt or uncle. The family cemetery plot, which had room for ten members, is now full. I visit often and recently cleaned the large angel with one hand raised toward heaven standing guard atop that thick Vermont stone with names of those who held family secrets.

It wasn't even three months later that we lost my brother Salvatore. He had two heart operations and completed therapy, but his heart was too weak to continue. He left behind his wife, Linda, son, Kenny, and grandson, Aiden. It was a miracle Sal survived his entry into this world. He was born in the backseat of a car on top of the Storm King Mountain in a snowstorm on the way to the hospital. He loved to sing with his church choir and for the holidays enjoyed performing the best "Dominic the Donkey." As one of my big brothers, Sal influenced my life in different ways. He taught me how to shoot basketball on our street with a rim attached to a telephone pole. He also instructed me on how to hit that speed bag hanging in the garage. When I was in high school and he was in the Army in Germany, he would write to me telling me to study and do my best in school. Right now as I update and edit this manuscript, I look over in my bookcase and can see Volume I and Volume II of Webster's Dictionary, very large editions that Sal sent to me from Germany.

Now my other two brothers and my sister are the old folks in the family. We are the aunts and uncles for the next generation of our children, nieces, and nephews to carry on. I don't have a cool cellar like my grandfather's with a barber chair. But I do have a secret "wine cellar" where I keep my vino at a cool temperature for our festivities. I hope our generation can experience and enjoy family gatherings with the next generation to give them the memories of their lifetime.

When I reviewed this manuscript, I discovered one thing that I did not even consider when I started to write down my thoughts, and that is death. I lost more than I realized when my family members, friends, coworkers, and even clients in the Program were no longer on this earth. It all seems so strange when you never know whose name is going into *The Book of Life*. I always kiss my wife and children and tell them I love them when we part.

One Christmas years ago, my brother Lee gave me *The Book of Italian Wisdom*.[8] I used some quotes from the small book in the opening chapters of this book. Lee had inscribed in that book, "Your roots are in Italy but your home is going to be in heaven."

I have shared some of the good, the bad, and the unique experiences in my life. If anything, I hope these pages will help our grandson, George Eden, understand and continue to embrace the ongoing heritage and culture of our Italian family, but more importantly I hope he is inspired to do his best. With God's blessing, he will have a life full of love and wonderful memories, and he will appreciate the sacrifices our immigrant parents made to give their children the freedom to choose a better life here in these great United States.

Acknowledgments

In the fall of 2013, our daughter Catherine and her husband, Paul, came to our house for a visit. Catherine told us she was expecting their first child. We were overjoyed and celebrated. Elaine had been asking me numerous times, "When are they going to have a baby?" Our prayers were answered! After they left and for the next few weeks, I started thinking about becoming a grandfather.

Around this same time of the year, a new mob book was published about a witness and his family who I interviewed for the Program. One day, Elaine and I were at a Barnes and Noble, where she was searching for a book. I walked over to the true crime section and saw the new mob book. I glanced through a few pages and noticed the name of the FBI case agent—Bob Marston.

When I got home later that day, I called Bob at home. He had been retired for a number of years. I knew Bob from working with him on the case. He told me he was interviewed numerous times for the book and stated, "You should have been in it" and "You could write your own book." We talked for a while. Bob reminded me of the time he and I had to go out to Long Island to check out a house that was owned by a relative of a witness. Afterward, we visited Teddy Roosevelt's house on Sagamore Hill. We had a good laugh that it was an enjoyable, beautiful afternoon.

After I hung up the phone, I started thinking about what Bob had said. I have to acknowledge it was Bob who first planted that seed in my mind. After I received permission to publish I called Bob. I informed him that I wrote a manuscript for a book that I was getting published and he was the one who first got me thinking about writing the book. He thought that was great!

At that time in 2013 when we learned we were going to have our first grandchild, I thought maybe it was time for my memoirs. I thought about my grandfather Sam, who passed away in 1968 at the age of eighty-seven. At that time, I was twenty-one years old and in the military. I started thinking, God willing, if I reach age eighty-seven, George Eden will also be twenty-one years old. I also started thinking about my father's dad, Gilberto, who passed away at the young age of fifty-two. At that time my father was only twenty-three years old. By writing my story I thought George Eden would have a better understanding of his grandfather's life and our family's history.

I had been retired for twelve years and I wanted to write about the journey I took down this road of life. This project was not just about me. In part, this book is the story of my immigrant parents' assimilation into American society. It is also about the assimilation of protected witnesses who made life-saving and life-changing decisions to enter the Witness Security Program and leave their life of crime. I have included some vignettes, some personal family memories, and some cultural aspects of the Italian-American experience.

All of the above could not have been accomplished without the assistance of my ever-supportive wife, Elaine. After I spent some time thinking about putting my thoughts into writing, I asked her what she thought. She was overjoyed, excited, and enthused. I advised her that we could not tell anyone until the time was right. I did not know if I would be authorized to write a book without the permission of the government.

So, for the next year or so, I would set aside time to gather my thoughts and write in longhand some of my experiences in different stages of my life. I enjoyed writing in the middle of the night when it was quiet and there were no distractions. Who better to have reviewing my manuscript than an English teacher with thirty-three years' teaching experience! Elaine was my early editor. Yes, we had disagreements and a lot of crumpled yellow sheets of paper thrown into the wastebasket.

One whole year went by and I was still in the early stages of my project. It was around my birthday, and Catherine and Theresa wanted to meet us in Brooklyn for dinner. Later that night I told them about *the book*! These were some of their reactions: "What! Mr. Secret, who never would tell us about his job, is going public!" "Dad, are you serious?" "What are you going to call it?" Of course, I had to also advise them not to say a word.

After I had completed a draft, they wanted to read it. We printed out three copies and I had a saved copy on the computer. We each had a copy in a binder. We agreed that each of them would review and make comments. It was a family effort. To this day, I cannot say enough about how helpful, insightful, and stimulating Elaine, Catherine, and Theresa were in assisting me in the creation of this work.

When Joe Montagna, former coworker at the Plaza and friend, would contact me, we often talked about our days at the Plaza. Our conversations refreshed my thoughts of those wonderful years in the hotel business. Even going back to that storied location further awakened my senses. In 2016, we met at the hotel and reminisced about the changes that have taken place there and in our own lives.

Thank you, Joe. Can't you smell the coffee brewing!

I also would like to thank Walter Mack and Dave Kelley. Two former AUSA's at SDNY. When I first started writing I reviewed my security agreement. I contacted them to discuss different options dealing with the Department of Justice. I thank them for their counsel.

After I submitted my manuscript to the government I explored different publishing methods while waiting for their response. I submitted numerous requests to small publishing companies. There was one publisher in Pennsylvania that I had a contract with. However, by the time the government approved my manuscript the publisher informed me that I would have to start the process at the end of the line. It would take another year to publish. As a result I decided to self-publish. I choose Outskirts Press. They have been very professional, responsible and timely in performing tasks that they inform me they will be conducting. I especially would like to thank the copywriter Reba, author representative Dana and all the other personnel at Outskirts.

Bibliography

[1]*Trentino Today, Provincia Autonoma di Trentino*, p.11, Provincia Autonoma di Trento. Published by Casa Editrice Panorama, Trento, Italy. All Rights Reserved.

[2]*Courthouses of the Second Circuit*, p. 35, Federal Bar Foundation. Acanthus Press. All Rights Reserved.

[3]*The Mafia of a Sicilian Village 1860–1960*, p. 143, Anton Blok, Harper & Row Publishers. All Rights Reserved.

[4]*The Italians*, Bantam Books, Luigi Barzini, pgs. 267, 268, 263, 264, 271, 273, 275. All Rights Reserved.

[5]*Little Italy*, Dr. Emelise Aleandri, p. 39, Arcadia Publishing. All Rights Reserved.

[6]"History of Val di Fiemme," *Filo Magazine*, PO Box 90, Crompond, New York 10517, p. 18. All Rights Reserved.

[7]"History of Enna," www.Sicilianexperience.com, p. 2; "Enna" p. 3; "Calascibetta," "Enna and Its Province" Azienda Provinciale Turismo, p. 9.

[8]*The Book of Italian Wisdom*, Antono Santi, Citadel Press, pgs.12, 46, 130, 138, 159, 191. Kensington Publishing Corporation. All Rights Reserved.

CPSIA information can be obtained
at www.ICGtesting.com
Printed in the USA
BVHW07s0831200718
522128BV00002B/10/P